OFFICIAL CIA MANUAL:
HUMAN RESOURCE EXPLOITATION TRAINING MANUAL

1982

Reprinted by PARANOIA PUBLISHING
http://www.paranoiamagazine.com

8 June 1988

The following Interrogation HRE training was provided by SAS/SOG/GB officers to countries in Latin America:

16-27 March 1987   GB officers provided a <u>multi-country</u> team two training to ███ possibly ███ and

March 1987   two GB officers (HRE)

16 Apr-4 May 84   two GB officers (HRE)

3-11 Nov 83   one GB officer (as part of the HRF program)

10-26 Oct 84   three GB officers (HRE)

25 Jul - 12 Aug 83   three GB officers (HRE)

Nov 82   two GB officers completed a site survey for HRE as part of the HRF program

DECL OADR
DRV HUM 4-82
CL BY ███████
ALL SECRET

INTERROGATION TEXT REVISIONS .

<u>Revision/Change</u>

A-2   Under D, last line, add the following:
                "We will discuss coercive techniques
                that have been used by many, and the
                reasons why we are against the use of
                these techniques".

A-6   Bottom of page: L. Change Bonafides
                to read "Verification";

B-3   Top of page: Ensure that the Instructor
                defines Liaison;

I-8   Bottom of page: Delete 7) Physical Violence;

K-1   Include in the introduction to Coercive
                Techniques:

                We will discuss some of those coercive
                techniques that have been used by many, and
                the reasons why we are against the use of
                these techniques.

                We do not use these techniques, nor do
                we condone the use of them.

Add the attached disclaimer, "Prohibition Against the Use
of Force", to the introduction. Reiterate when discussing
Non-Coercive and Coercive techniques. Ensure that the students
understand our position.

TABLE OF CONTENTS

NOTE:
Letter and digit(s) in left margin are slide numbers

PROHIBITION AGAINST USE OF FORCE

The use of force, mental torture, threats, insults, or exposure to unpleasant and inhumane treatment of any kind as an aid to interrogation is prohibited by law, both international and domestic; it is neither authorized nor condoned. The interrogator must <u>never</u> take advantage of the source's weaknesses to the extent that the interrogation involves threats, insults, torture or exposure to unpleasant or inhumane treatment of any kind. Experience indicates that the use of force is not necessary to gain cooperation of sources. Use of force is a poor technique, yields unreliable results, may damage subsequent collection efforts, and can induce the source to say what he thinks the interrogator wants to hear. Additionally, the use of force will probably result in adverse publicity and/or legal action against the interrogator (et. al) when the source is released. However, the use of force is not to be confused with psychological ploys, verbal trickery, or other nonviolent and non-coercive ruses employed by the interrogator in the successful interrogation of reticent or uncooperative sources.

INTRODUCTION

I.   OPENING REMARKS

A.   THERE IS NOTHING MYSTERIOUS ABOUT "QUESTIONING". IT IS NO MORE THAN OBTAINING NEEDED INFORMATION FROM SUBJECTS. THESE MAY BE PRISONERS OF WAR. DEFECTORS. REFUGEES, ILLEGAL IMMIGRANTS, AGENTS OR SUSPECTED INTELLIGENCE AGENTS ATTEMPTING TO OPERATE IN YOUR COUNTRY.

B.   THE ART OF "QUESTIONING" HAS BECOME CONTROVERSIAL IN MANY PARTS OF THE WORLD. THIS IS BECAUSE IN MANY COUNTRIES, THE TERM "QUESTIONING" HAS BEEN IDENTIFIED WITH THE USE OF TORTURE TO OBTAIN INFORMATION.

EVERY MANUAL I HAVE READ ON "QUESTIONING" STATES THAT INFORMATION OBTAINED FROM A SUBJECT UNDER TORTURE IS NOT RELIABLE. THAT THE SUBJECT WILL SAY WHATEVER HE THINKS YOU WANT TO HEAR JUST TO AVOID FURTHER PUNISHMENT.

DURING THE BATTLE OF ALGIERS. THE FRENCH ARMY USED TORTURE TO NEUTRALIZE A TERRORIST GROUP WITHIN A MATTER OF MONTHS. UNFORTUNATELY. ALONG WITH THE HUNDREDS OF TERRORISTS THAT WERE ARRESTED AND TORTURED. SO WERE HUNDREDS OF INNOCENT CIVILIANS. SOCIETY SIMPLY WILL NOT CONDONE THIS.

C. THE ROUTINE USE OF TORTURE LOWERS THE MORAL

CALIBER OF THE ORGANIZATION THAT USES IT AND CORRUPTS

THOSE THAT RELY ON IT AS THE QUICK AND EASY WAY OUT.

WE STRONGLY DISAGREE WITH THIS APPROACH AND INSTEAD

EMPHASIZE THE USE .OF PSYCHOLOGICAL TECHNIQUES DESIGNED

TO PERSUADE THE SUBJECT TO WANT TO FURNISH US WITH THE

INFORMATION WE DESIRE.

D. SUCCESSFUL "QUESTIONING" IS BASED UPON A

KNOWLEDGE OF THE SUBJECT MATTER AND UPON THE USE OF

PSYCHOLOGICAL TECHNIQUES WHICH ARE NOT DIFFICULT TO

UNDERSTAND. WE WILL BE DISCUSSING TWO TYPES OF

TECHNIQUES, COERCIVE AND NON-COERCIVE. WHILE WE ~~DO~~
DEPLORE
. ~~DISCUSSED~~ THE USE OF COERCIVE TECHNIQUES, WE DO WANT.
                              SO THAT YOU MAY AVOID
TO MAKE YOU AWARE OF THEM ~~AND THE PROPER WAY TO USE~~

THEM.

E. PSYCHOLOGISTS HAVE CONDUCTED CONSIDERABLE

RESEARCH IN MANY AREAS THAT ARE CLOSELY RELATED .TO

·COERCIVE "QUESTIONING". DURING THIS COURSE WE WILL

DISCUSS THE FOLLOWING TOPICS AS THEY RELATE TO

"QUESTIONING":

    1. REACTIONS. TO PAIN AND FEAR.

    2. THE EFFECTS OF DEBILITY AND ISOLATION.

    3. HYPNOSIS AND NARCOSIS

F.   WHAT WE ARE EMPHASIZING THROUGHOUT THIS COURSE IS THAT "QUESTIONING" IS A COMPLICATED PROCESS INVOLVING THE INTERACTION OF TWO PERSONALITIES — THAT OF THE QUESTIONER AND THAT OF THE SUBJECT.   IT MUST BE WELL PLANNED — FROM THE TIME THE SUBJECT IS ARRESTED THROUGH THE QUESTIONING PROCESS TO THE FINAL DISPOSITION OF THE SUBJECT.

II.   ADMINISTRATIVE DETAILS

A.   SCHEDULE AND HOURS

   1.   TWO WEEKS OF LECTURES IN THE CLASSROOM

   2.   ONE OR TWO WEEKS OF PRACTICAL WORK WITH PRISONERS, AT WHICH TIME THE CLASS WILL BE DIVIDED INTO 3 OR 4 MAN TEAMS.

B.   SCOPE OF INSTRUCTION

   1.   THE INTELLIGENCE CYCLE

   2.   LIAISON RELATIONSHIPS

   3.   USE OF INTERPRETERS

   4.   SELECTION OF "QUESTIONERS"

   5.   DESIGN & MANAGEMENT OF A FACILITY

   6.   ARREST & HANDLING OF SUBJECTS

   7.   PSYCHOLOGICAL ASSESMENT OF SUBJECTS

   8.   PRINCIPLES FOR PLANNING & CONDUCTING THE "QUESTIONING"

   9.   NON-COERCIVE "QUESTIONING" TECHNIQUES

   10.   COERCIVE "QUESTIONING" TECHNIQUES AND THEY SHOULD NOT BE USED.

   11.   REPORT WRITING

C.   STUDENT QUESTIONS OR COMMENTS

FEEL FREE TO MAKE COMMENTS, RELATE PERSONAL

EXPERIENCES, OR ASK QUESTIONS AT ANY TIME DURING

THE COURSE.   OCCASIONALLY WE MAY ONLY GIVE YOU A

BRIEF ANSWER BECAUSE SOME TOPICS WILL BE MORE

FULLY COVERED DURING A LATER CLASS.

D.   USE OF VIDEO CAMERA

WE WILL BE VIDEO RECORDING PORTIONS OF YOUR

PRACTICAL EXCERCISES.   THE VIDEO NOT ONLY ALLOWS

YOU TO REVIEW YOUR QUESTIONING TECHNIQUES BUT

ALSO TO STUDY THE REACTIONS OF THE SUBJECTS

DURING THE QUESTIONING.

III. DEFINITIONS

TO INSURE THAT WE ALL UNDERSTAND THE TERMS WHICH WE

WILL BE USING THROUGHOUT THE COURSE HERE ARE A FEW

DEFINITIONS:

A-1   A.   INFORMATION - RAW DATA WHICH IS OBTAINED FROM A

VARIETY OF SOURCES: RUMORS. INFORMANTS. PRISONERS,

ETC.   IT MAY BE ACCURATE OR INACCURATE.

A-2   INTELLIGENCE - THE RESULT OF AN ANALYSIS OF ALL

THE INFORMATION OBTAINED CONCERNING A GIVEN SUBJECT.

A-3   C.   "QUESTIONING" – OBTAINING INFORMATION BY DIRECT QUESTIONING OF A PERSON UNDER CONDITIONS FULLY OR PARTIALLY CONTROLLED BY THE "QUESTIONER". OR BELIEVED BY THAT PERSON TO BE UNDER THE "QUESTIONER'S" CONTROL. "QUESTIONING" IS USUALLY RESERVED FOR SUBJECTS WHO ARE SUSPECT, RESISTANT OR BOTH.

A-4   D.   "QUESTIONER" – A PERSON TRAINED AND EXPERIENCED IN THE ART OF EXTRACTING INFORMATION FROM A SUBJECT IN RESPONSE TO EXPLICIT REQUIREMENTS.   THE SUBJECT MAY BE EITHER COOPERATIVE OR RESISTANT.

A-5   "QUESTIONING" FACILITY – A BUILDING OR SERIES OF BUILDINGS DESIGNED TO ENHANCE DETENTION AND "QUESTIONING" OF SUBJECTS WITH A VIEW TOWARD OBTAINING MAXIMUM COOPERATION.   THIS WILL INCLUDE ENVIRONMENTAL. PHYSICAL AND PSYCHOLOGICAL CONTROLS.

A-6   F.   INTERVIEW – OBTAINING INFORMATION. NOT USUALLY UNDER CONTROLLED CONDITIONS. BY QUESTIONING A PERSON WHO IS AWARE OF THE NATURE AND SIGNIFICANCE OF HIS ANSWERS BUT NOT AWARE OF THE SPECIFIC PURPOSE OF THE INTERVIEWER.

A-7   G.   DEBRIEFING – OBTAINING INFORMATION BY QUESTIONING A CONTROLLED. AND SOMETIMES WITTING. SUBJECT WHO IS NORMALLY WILLING TO PROVIDE THE DESIRED INFORMATION.

A-8   H.   ELICITATION – OBTAINING INFORMATION WITHOUT
REVEALING THE INTENT OR EXCEPTIONAL INTEREST OF THE
QUESTIONER, THROUGH A VERBAL OR WRITTEN EXCHANGE WITH
A SUBJECT WHO MAY OR MAY NOT BE WILLING TO PROVIDE IT
IF HE KNEW THE TRUE PURPOSE.

A-9   I.   CONTROL – THE CAPACITY TO CAUSE OR CHANGE CERTAIN
TYPES OF HUMAN BEHAVIOR BY IMPLYING OR USING PHYSICAL
OR PSYCHOLOGICAL MEANS TO INDUCE COMPLIANCE.
COMPLIANCE MAY BE VOLUNTARY OR INVOLUNTARY.

CONTROL CAN RARELY BE ESTABLISHED WITHOUT CONTROL OF
THE ENVIRONMENT. BY CONTROLLING THE SUBJECT'S
PHYSICAL ENVIRONMENT, WE WILL BE ABLE TO CONTROL HIS
PSYCHOLOGICAL STATE OF MIND.

A-10   J.   REQUIREMENTS – THE WRITTEN DETAILED DEMAND FROM
VARIOUS CUSTOMER AGENCIES FOR SPECIFIC INFORMATION OR
FOR SPOTTING OF POTENTIAL ASSETS.

A-11   K.   SUBJECT – A PERSON BELIEVED TO POSSESS
INFORMATION OF VALUE TO THE SERVICE QUESTIONING HIM.

A-12   L.   BONAFIDES – EVIDENCE OR RELIABLE INFORMATION
REGARDING A SUBJECT'S IDENTITY, PERSONAL HISTORY, AND
INTENTIONS OF GOOD FAITH.

A-13   M.   SCREENING – THE PRELIMINARY INTERVIEWING OF A
SUBJECT TO OBTAIN BIOGRAPHIC AND OTHER BACKGROUND
INFORMATION.

A-17   COLLECTION

              THIS IS WHERE "QUESTIONING" FITS INTO THE CYCLE.

A-18   COLLECTION ALSO INCLUDES OTHER SOURCES SUCH AS:

              RESEARCH, BOOKS AND MAGAZINES, PICTURES,

              NEWSPAPERS, ETC. COLLECTION ONLY PRODUCES

              INFORMATION, NOT INTELLIGENCE.

A-19.   C.   PROCESSING

              IN ORDER TO BE PROCESSED, THE INFORMATION MUST BE

A-20   ACCURATELY RECORDED. THEN IT MUST BE EVALUATED

              AS TO ITS RELEVANCE TO THE REQUIREMENTS AND THE

              RELIABILITY OF THE SOURCE. LASTLY IT MUST BE

              ANALYZED TO DETERMINE ITS SIGNIFICANCE WITH

              RESPECT TO OTHER INFORMATION ABOUT THE SAME TOPIC.

A-21   D.   DISSEMINATION
  &   --------------
A-22   THE PROCESSED INFORMATION IS NOW INTELLIGENCE AND

              MUST BE DISSEMINATED IN A TIMELY MANER TO SOMEONE

              WHO CAN ACT UPON IT. THE INTELLIGENCE REPORT

              WHICH IS DISSEMINATED WILL THEN GENERATE

              REQUIREMENTS FOR ADDITIONAL INFORMATION AND THE

              CYCLE BEGINS ALL OVER AGAIN.

A-14   N.   ASSESSMENT — THE ANALYSIS OF THE PSYCHOLOGICAL

AND BIOGRAPHICAL DATA ABOUT A SUBJECT FOR THE PURPOSE

OF MAKING AN APPRAISAL.   THE SPECIFIC TECHNIQUES WHICH

WILL BE USED DURING THE "QUESTIONING" WILL DEPEND UPON

THE ASSESSMENT.

A-15 IV. THE CYCLE OF INTELLIGENCE

           THE INTELLIGENCE CYCLE CONSISTS OF FOUR PHASES AND CAN

BE REPRESENTED AS A CIRCLE BECAUSE IT HAS NO BEGINNING

OR END.

A-16   A.   REQUIREMENTS

             THE DEMAND FOR CERTAIN TYPES OF INFORMATION

             ESTABLISHES PURPOSE AND DIRECTION FOR CONDUCTING

             THE "QUESTIONING".   THERE ARE TWO TYPES OF

             REQUIREMENTS:

A-16   1.   STANDING REQUIREMENTS — e.g. INFORMATION

             CONCERNING THREATS AGAINST GOVERNMENT OFFICIALS,

             SUBVERSIVE GROUPS, TERRORIST ACTIONS, ARMED

             ATTACK.

A-16   SPECIFIC REQUIREMENTS — e.g. INFORMATION

             CONCERNING A TOPIC ABOUT WHICH A SUBJECT HAS

             SPECIALIZED KNOWLEDGE, SUCH AS SCIENTIFIC OR

             TECHNICAL KNOWLEDGE.

B-0

B-1   I.   LEGAL CONSIDERATIONS
             -------------- .---

THE LEGALITY OF DETAINING AND "QUESTIONING" A SUBJECT,
AND OF THE METHODS EMPLOYED. IS DETERMINED BY THE LAWS
OF THE COUNTRY IN WHICH IT IS DONE. IT IS THEREFORE
IMPORTANT THAT ALL "QUESTIONERS" AND THEIR SUPERVISORS
BE FULLY AND ACCURATELY INFORMED ABOUT THE APPLICABLE
LOCAL LAWS.

DO NOT ASSUME THAT ALL MEMBERS OF A LIAISON SERVICE
KNOW THE PERTINENT STATUTES. IT IS RECOMMENDED THAT
COPIES OR LEGAL EXTRACTS OF ALL APPLICABLE LAWS BE
KEPT IN A SEPARATE FILE AND THAT ALL "QUESTIONERS"
REREAD. THE FILE PERIODICALLY.

IT IS THE RESPONSIBILITY OF THE "QUESTIONER" TO BE
SURE THAT THE "QUESTIONING" IS LEGAL. WHETHER IT IS
CONDUCTED UNILATERALLY OR JOINTLY. A JOINT ILLEGAL
"QUESTIONING" MAY LATER EMBARRASS BOTH SERVICES AND
LEAD TO RECRIMINATIONS AND STRAINED RELATIONS BETWEEN
THEM.

DETENTION POSES THE MOST COMMON OF THE LEGAL PROBLEMS.
DETENTION IN A CONTROLLED ENVIRONMENT AND PERHAPS FOR
A LENGTHY PERIOD IS FREQUENTLY ESSENTIAL TO A
SUCCESSFUL "QUESTIONING" OF A RESISTANT SUBJECT. SOME
SECURITY SERVICES MAY WORK AT THEIR LEISURE, RELYING
UPON TIME AS WELL AS METHODS TO MELT RESISTANCE. THE
CHOICE OF METHODS DEPENDS IN LARGE PART UPON HOW LONG
THE SUBJECT CAN BE LEGALLY DETAINED.

FACTORS RELATING TO THE LEGALITY OF THE "QUESTIONING":

B-1   A.   DOES SERVICE HAVE LAW ENFORCEMENT POWERS?

B-2   B.   DOES SERVICE HAVE AUTHORITY TO OPERATE IN HOME
COUNTRY?

B-3   C.   DOES "QUESTIONING" OF CITIZENS REQUIRE SPECIAL
APPROVAL?

B-4   D.   ILLEGAL DETENTION ALWAYS REQUIRES PRIOR HQS
APPROVAL.

B-5   E.   COERCIVE TECHNIQUES ~~ALWAYS REQUIRE PRIOR HQS~~
~~APPROVAL.~~ CONSTITUTE AN IMPROPRIETY AND
VIOLATE POLICY.

B-6   II.   ADVANTAGES OF WORKING WITH LIAISON

B-6   A.   HAS THE LEGAL ATHORITY TO DETAIN AND "QUESTION".

B-7   B.   CAN PROVIDE NECESSARY DETENTION FACILITIES.

B-8   C.   HAS THE ABILITY TO FOLLOW UP ON OPERATIONAL LEADS.

B-9   D.   CAN PROVIDE SUPPORT PERSONNEL SUCH AS: GUARDS,
                    DRIVERS, INTERPRETERS, MEDICAL AND HOUSEKEEPING
                    PERSONNEL.

B-10   E.   CAN PROVIDE EASY ACCESS TO LIAISON FILES.
                    - TO VERIFY INFORMATION OBTAINED FROM THE SUBJECT.
                    - TO PROVIDE ADDITIONAL INFORMATION YOU MAY NOT
                    HAVE (e.g. GIVE US A NAME AND D.O.B. AND WE CAN
                    PROVIDE YOU WITH A COMPUTERIZED PERSONAL HISTORY
                    OF THE SUBJECT).

              IT IS ALSO IMPORTANT TO MAINTAIN LIAISON WITH OTHER
              GOVERNMENT AGENCIES WITHIN YOUR OWN COUNTRY. FOR
              EXAMPLE, IN THE U.S. EACH STATE AND FEDERAL LAW
              ENFORCEMENT AGENCY HAS ITS OWN COMPUTERIZED DATA BASE.
              EACH AGENCY SHARES ITS INFORMATION WITH ALL THE OTHERS
              BY CONNECTING TO A CENTRALIZED COMPUTER. FROM ONE
              TERMINAL IN OUR OFFICE WE CAN ACCESS N.C.I.C.,
              T.C.I.C., T.E.C.S., N.L.E.T.S., ETC.

B-11   III.   DISADVANTAGES OF WORKING WITH LIAISON

B-11   .A.   LACK OF UNDERSTANDING OF THE VALUE OF

"QUESTIONING" IN THE INTELLIGENCE CYCLE.

B-12   B.   LACK OF TRAINING AND EXPERIENCE IN "QUESTIONING

B-13   C.

B-14   D.

B-15   E.   HOSTILE PENETRATION OF THE LIAISON SERVICE.

B-16   F.   TENDENCY TO WITHHOLD INFORMATION OR SOURCES.

B-17   G.   LIMITATIONS IMPOSED ON COOPERATION FOR POLITICAL

REASONS. *PROHIBITION AGAINST OUR DIRECT ARTICIPATION*

H. *IN LIAISON QUESTIONING EXCEPT WITH PRIOR*

ONE CAUTION ABOUT WORKING WITH ANOTHER SERVICE: BE *HIGH LEVEL*

SURE THAT THE OTHER SERVICE WILL MAINTAIN YOUR *HQS APPROVAL*

SECURITY AND THAT OF THE SUBJECT.

INTERPRETERS
========-----

I. INTRODUCTION

THERE WILL BE MANY OCCASIONS WHEN BORDER CROSSERS,

REFUGEES, PRISONERS OF WAR, SUSPECTED AGENTS, OR OTHER

POTENTIAL SUBJECTS FOR "QUESTIONING" WILL NOT SPEAK

YOUR NATIVE LANGUAGE. THEREFORE, THE USE OF AN

INTERPRETER MAY BE ESSENTIAL TO SUCCESSFULLY COMPLETE

AN EXPLOITATION.

WHEN USED PROPERLY, AN INTERPRETER CAN BE YOUR KEY

ASSISTANT IN PERFORMING YOUR DUTIES AND A CONTROL TO

HELP YOU AVOID VIOLATING CUSTOMS AND TRADITIONS.

HOWEVER, PLEASE KEEP IN MIND THAT THE USE OF AN

INTERPRETER MUST NEVER BE CONSIDERED A SATISFACTORY

SUBSTITUTE FOR DIRECT COMMUNICATION BETWEEN YOU AND

THE SUBJECT.

II. DIFFICULTIES & LIMITATIONS

C-1   A: THE AMOUNT OF TIME REQUIRED TO CONDUCT THE

"QUESTIONING" WILL MORE THAN DOUBLE.

C-2   YOU WILL EXPERIENCE CONSIDERABLE DIFFICULTY IN

TRYING TO ESTABLISH RAPPORT WITH THE SUBJECT BECAUSE

OF THE LACK OF PERSONAL CONTACT, THAT IS, NOT BEING

ABLE TO SPEAK DIRECTLY TO THE INDIVIDUAL.

C-3   IT IS EXTREMELY DIFFICULT TO USE CERTAIN
"QUESTIONING" TECHNIQUES, SUCH AS RAPID FIRE
QUESTIONING, WHEN USING AN INTERPRETER.

C-4   D.   CERTAIN MEANINGS, TONAL INFLECTIONS, AND
EXPRESSIONS ARE ALMOST IMPOSSIBLE TO CONVEY TO THE
SUBJECT THROUGH AN INTERPRETER. THIS INCREASES THE
POSSIBILITY OF MISUNDERSTANDINGS.

C-5   E.   THE PRESENCE OF AN INTERPRETER MAY CAUSE AN
OTHERWISE COOPERATIVE SUBJECT TO WITHHOLD INFORMATION
DURING THE "QUESTIONING". SOME SUBJECTS ARE WILLING
TO GIVE INFORMATION ONLY IF THEY CAN BE SURE THAT
THEIR OWN FORCES WILL NOT FIND OUT THAT THEY TALKED,
THAT THERE WILL BE NO RETRIBUTION. THE PRESENCE OF
ANY THIRD PARTY AT THE "QUESTIONING", EVEN AN
INTERPRETER, MAY CAUSE THE SUBJECT TO DOUBT THIS
ASSURANCE.

C-6   F.   THERE IS A SECURITY RISK POSED BECAUSE THE
INTERPRETER IS JUST ONE MORE INDIVIDUAL TO BECOME
AWARE OF INTELLIGENCE REQUIREMENTS, AND HE WILL OBTAIN
CONSIDERABLE INFORMATION OF A CLASSIFIED NATURE DURING
THE COURSE OF THE "QUESTIONING".

III. SELECTION OF INTERPRETERS

FROM A SECURITY STANDPOINT, INTERPRETERS SHOULD BE SELECTED FROM YOUR OWN SERVICES, OR AT LEAST YOUR NATIONALITY, IF AT ALL POSSIBLE. IN SOME INSTANCES, HOWEVER, IT WILL BE NECESSARY TO HIRE OR USE FOREIGNERS FOR THIS PURPOSE. LET'S DISCUSS SOME OF THE FACTORS WHICH MUST BE CONSIDERED WHEN SELECTING AN INTERPRETER.

C-7

A. SECURITY CLEARANCE

IT IS IMPORTANT THAT AN INTERPRETER HAVE A SECURITY CLEARANCE BECAUSE OF THE OPPOSITION'S CONTINUED EFFORTS TO PENETRATE YOUR ORGANIZATION AND LEARN YOUR INTELLIGENCE REQUIREMENTS.

C-8

B. LANGUAGE CAPABILITY

HE SHOULD BE COMPLETELY FLUENT IN YOUR LANGUAGE AS WELL AS THE LANGUAGE OF THE SUBJECT. THIS IS VERY IMPORTANT IN BOTH SPEAKING THESE LANGUAGES AND WRITING THEM.

C-9

C. PERSONALITY

WHENEVER POSSIBLE, THE PERSONALITY OF THE INTERPRETER SHOULD BE THE SAME OR NEARLY THE SAME AS YOURS. THIS WILL OFTEN COME ABOUT AS THE TWO OF YOU WORK TOGETHER MORE AND MORE OFTEN. IF THERE ARE SERIOUS PERSONALITY DIFFERENCES BETWEEN THE TWO OF YOU, YOU SHOULD GET ANOTHER INTERPRETER.

THE INTERPRETER SHOULD BE ABLE TO ADJUST HIS
PERSONALITY TO THAT OF THE SUBJECT, AND TO THE
"QUESTIONING" TECHNIQUES BEING USED.

C-10   D.   SOCIAL STATUS

THIS IS ALWAYS A CONSIDERATION IN THOSE COUNTRIES
IN WHICH SOCIAL STATUS EXISTS. IN A LIAISON
SITUATION BE SURE THE INTERPRETER HAS THE SOCIAL
STATURE FOR CONTACT WITH THE OFFICIALS WITH WHOM
HE WILL BE TALKING.

DURING THE "QUESTIONING" OF A SUBJECT IN WHICH A
DIFFERENCE OF CLASSES MAY EXIST BETWEEN THE
SUBJECT AND THE INTERPRETER, YOU MUST MAKE IT
CLEAR TO THE SUBJECT THAT THE CONVERSATION IS
STRICTLY BETWEEN THE TWO OF YOU, THAT THE
INTERPRETER IS SIMPLY A DEVICE FOR CONVERTING THE
LANGUAGE.

IN CERTAIN SOCIETIES WOMEN ARE OFTEN VIEWED AS
HAVING INFERIOR SOCIAL STATUS AND USING A FEMALE
INTERPRETER MAY NOT BE ADVISABLE IN CASES WHERE A
MAN IS BEING "QUESTIONED".

THE CHANGE IN TONAL INFLECTIONS AS A FEMALE
INTERPRETS THE QUESTIONS OF A MALE "QUESTIONER"
CAUSES THE EFFECT TO BE LOSS DURING TRANSLATION.
ACCORDING TO PSYCHOLOGICAL TESTS, MEN AND WOMEN
BOTH RESPOND BETTER TO QUESTIONING BY A MALE.

C-11

E.   SOURCES OF INTERPRETERS

MOST SECURITY SERVICES ALREADY HAVE EXISTING

C-12

INTERPRETER POOLS FROM WHICH YOU CAN SELECT

SOMEONE WHO MEETS YOUR REQUIREMENTS.

2.

C-12

WHO NO LONGER HAS A NEED FOR

HIM.

THAT YOU FULLY UNDERSTAND WHY THE

OTHER OFFICER IS WILLING TO RELEASE HIM.

Slide
C-15

AND THE OTHER OFFICER UNDERSTAND

THAT THERE ARE TO BE NO RESIDUAL RELATIONSHIPS

BETWEEN THEM.

THAT NO TWO OFFICERS WILL USE AN

INTERPRETER IN EXACTLY THE SAME FASHION.

THAT YOU PLAN TO CHANGE ANY OF HIS

HABITS WHICH YOU CONSIDER UNDESIREABLE.

C-12

3.   IT MAY BE NECESSARY TO USE AN INTERPRETER

FROM A SOURCE OUTSIDE YOUR OWN SERVICE.

EDUCATIONAL FACILITIES ARE AN EXCELLENT SOURCE

FOR NEW TALENT.

GENERAL SUGGESTIONS

C-13

C-14   F.

1. WAIT UNTIL YOU HAVE SEVERAL LEADS BEFORE INTERVIEWING ANY CANDIDATES.

C-14   2. INTERVIEW ALL SERIOUS CANDIDATES.

C-14   3. RUN TRACES ON ALL CANDIDATES, THROUGH BOTH YOUR OWN AND LIAISON SERVICES.

C-14   4. REVIEW ALL PERSONNEL FILES THOROUGHLY ON EACH CANDIDATE, INCLUDING ANY PERFORMANCE REPORTS.

C-14   5. LAY OUT ALL GROUND RULES AT THE TIME OF RECRUITMENT. BE SURE HE UNDERSTANDS ALL CONDITIONS OF EMPLOYMENT, SUCH AS SALARY AND BENEFITS, AND WHAT HE WILL OR WILL NOT BE ENTITLED TO.

C-14   6. INSOFAR AS POSSIBLE, HAVE ALL UNDERSTANDINGS IN WRITING.

C-14   7. BE ESPECIALLY WATCHFUL FOR ATTEMPTS TO PENETRATE YOUR OFFICE.

C-15 --------- Return to E. 2., p. C-5

C-16 IV. TRAINING OF INTERPRETERS

C-16 A. ESTABLISH YOUR AUTHORITY AS SOON AS POSSIBLE AND
BE SURE THE INTERPRETER UNDERSTANDS THE LIMITS OF HIS
AUTHORITY. YOU ARE RESPONSIBLE FOR INSTRUCTING THE
INTERPRETER IN HIS DUTIES, THE STANDARDS OF CONDUCT
EXPECTED FROM HIM, THE TECHNIQUES TO BE USED DURING
"QUESTIONING", AND ANY OTHER REQUIREMENTS WHICH YOU
CONSIDER NECESSARY.

C-17 B. DETERMINE HIS CURRENT LEVEL OF TRAINING AND
EXPERIENCE, NOTING ANY UNDESIREABLE CHARACTERISTICS OR
HABITS. NOTIFY HIM FIRMLY OF ANY CHARACTERISTICS YOU
WANT CHANGED AND HOW TO DO IT.

IF POSSIBLE, HAVE A NEW INTERPRETER UNDERSTUDY
ONE WHO IS ALREADY PROFICIENT, OR AT LEAST AFFORD HIM
THE OPPORTUNITY TO PRACTICE SKILLS LEARNED UNDER
SUPERVISION.

C-18 C. ACCURACY OF TRANSLATIONS SHOULD BE STRESSED. HE
MUST REALIZE THAT IF HE DOES NOT UNDERSTAND WHAT YOU
ARE TRYING TO SAY, HE SHOULD NOT TRY TO FAKE IT, BUT
SHOULD FIRST DISCUSS IT WITH YOU BEFORE INTERPRETING.

HE SHOULD BE MADE TO UNDERSTAND THAT HE IS YOUR
"RIGHT HAND" OR "MOUTHPIECE" AND IS INDISPENSIBLE TO
THE "QUESTIONING". HOWEVER, HE MUST BE CAUTIONED NOT
TO INTERJECT HIS OWN IDEAS INTO THE "QUESTIONING". HE
SHOULD TRANSLATE DIRECTLY ANY STATEMENTS MADE BY YOU
OR THE SUBJECT.

HE SHOULD AVOID SUCH EXPRESSIONS AS "HE WANTS TO KNOW IF YOU...." OR "HE SAID TO TELL YOU THAT....", ETC.

C-19   D.   PERIODIC TESTING AND EVALUATION OF THE INTERPRETER SHOULD BE CONDUCTED THROUGH TAPES OR WRITING. THIS SHOULD BE DONE WITHOUT HIS KNOWING THAT HE IS BEING EVALUATED.

C-20   E.   SPECIAL ATTENTION SHOULD BE GIVEN TO THE DEVELOPMENT OF LANGUAGE PROFICIENCY IN THE TECHNICAL FIELDS IN WHICH THE INTERPRETER WILL BE USED. THE USE OF TECHNICAL TERMS WILL GREATLY INCREASE THE COMPLEXITY OF THE QUESTIONS ASKED AND ANSWERS GIVEN. THEREFORE, THE INTERPRETER MUST UNDERSTAND THE SUBJECT MATTER ALMOST AS WELL AS YOU DO.

C-21   F.   MAKE IT CLEAR TO THE INTERPRETER THAT THE QUANTITY AND QUALITY OF INFORMATION OBTAINED DURING THE "QUESTIONING" WILL DEPEND UPON HIS ABILITY AS AN INTERPRETER.

C-22   V.   USE OF INTERPRETERS

THE PROCEDURES TO BE USED DURING "QUESTIONING" MUST BE ADAPTED TO THE USE OF AN INTERPRETER. SOME OF THESE ADAPTATIONS NEED ONLY BE CONSIDERED THE FIRST TIME YOU USE A PARTICULAR INTERPRETER. THEY DO NOT NEED TO BE RECONSIDERED IF THE TWO OF YOU CONSTANTLY WORK TOGETHER AS A TEAM.

A. PLANNING AND PREPARATION

ALWAYS THOROUGHLY BRIEF THE INTERPRETER ON ANY

AND ALL INFORMATION AVAILABLE REGARDING THE

SUBJECT AND THE OBJECTIVES OF THE "QUESTIONING".

PRIOR TO THE START OF THE "QUESTIONING", THE

INTERPRETER SHOULD BE GIVEN THE OPPORTUNITY TO

CONDUCT ANY NECESSARY RESEARCH CONCERNING

TECHNICAL OR PROFESSIONAL TERMS TO BE USED DURING

THE "QUESTIONING". IN SOME CASES IT WILL BE

NECESSARY FOR YOU TO PROVIDE HIM WITH A PRECISE

DEFINITION OF THE TERMS YOU PLAN TO USE TO ENSURE

A CLEAR UNDERSTANDING BY THE INTERPRETER.

B. PHYSICAL ARRANGEMENTS

INSTRUCT THE INTERPRETER ON THE PHYSICAL

ARRANGEMENTS FOR THE "QUESTIONING". HE SHOULD

SEE THE ACTUAL FACILITIES TO BE USED AND SHOULD

KNOW EXACTLY WHERE HIS PHYSICAL POSITION WILL BE

IN RELATION TO YOU AND THE SUBJECT. THE MOST

DESIREABLE ARRANGEMENT IS FOR YOU AND THE SUBJECT

TO FACE EACH OTHER ACROSS OPPOSITE SIDES OF A

TABLE WITH THE INTERPRETER LOCATED AT ONE END OF

THE TABLE.

C. METHOD OF INTERPRETATION

SELECT THE METHOD OF INTERPRETATION TO BE USED DURING THE "QUESTIONING", THAT IS, EITHER THE ALTERNATE OR THE SIMULTANEOUS METHOD. THIS CHOICE SHOULD BE BASED UPON YOUR EVALUATION OF THE INTERPRETER'S ABILITY AND PERSONAL CHARACTERISTICS. EACH METHOD HAS CERTAIN ADVANTAGES AND DISADVANTAGES OF WHICH YOU SHOULD BE AWARE.

ALTERNATE METHOD

IN THIS METHOD, YOU SPEAK ENTIRE THOUGHTS, SENTENCES, AND SOMETIMES EVEN PARAGRAPHS, AND THEN WAIT FOR THE INTERPRETER TO TRANSLATE ALL THAT HAS BEEN SAID. THIS REQUIRES THE INTERPRETER TO HAVE AN EXCEPTIONALLY GOOD MEMORY, BUT DOES ALLOW HIM TO REPHRASE STATEMENTS TO ENSURE BETTER UNDERSTANDING IN THE SECOND LANGUAGE. THIS IS IMPORTANT WHEN THE SENTENCE STRUCTURE OF THE SUBJECT'S LANGUAGE DIFFERS FROM THAT OF YOUR OWN LANGUAGE.

THE ALTERNATE METHOD HAS THE DISADVANTAGE OF MAKING THE INTERPRETER'S PRESENCE MORE EVIDENT OR OBVIOUS. THIS TENDS TO BREAK DOWN THE EYE-TO-EYE CONTACT THAT IS DESIRED BETWEEN YOU AND THE SUBJECT.

SIMULTANEOUS METHOD

IN THIS METHOD, THE INTERPRETER TRANSLATES YOUR WORDS AS YOU ARE SPEAKING, KEEPING UP WITH YOU AS CLOSELY AS POSSIBLE, USUALLY ONLY A FEW WORDS OR A PHRASE BEHIND. THIS ALLOWS HIM TO MORE ACCURATELY CONVEY THE EXACT MENTAL ATTITUDE AND FINE SHADES OF MEANING WHICH YOU OR THE SUBJECT ARE TRYING TO EXPRESS. BECAUSE THERE ARE NO LONG PAUSES DURING WHICH YOU OR THE SUBJECT ARE NOT INVOLVED, THIS METHOD PROMOTES ATTENTIVE LISTENING AND INCREASES THE RAPPORT BETWEEN YOU AND THE SUBJECT.

THE SIMULTANEOUS METHOD HAS THE DISADVANTAGE OF GREATER CHANCE OF ERROR DURING INTERPRETING, ESPECIALLY WHERE THERE IS A DIFFERENCE IN SENTENCE STRUCTURE BETWEEN THE TWO LANGUAGES. IT ALSO REQUIRES A VERY HIGH DEGREE OF PROFICIENCY IN BOTH LANGUAGES.

D. TECHNIQUES TO BE USED

INSTRUCT THE INTERPRETER ON THE MANNER IN WHICH

THE "QUESTIONING" IS TO TAKE PLACE AND TECHNIQUES

TO BE USED. IF POSSIBLE, YOU SHOULD PRACTICE

WITH HIM UNDER CONDITIONS AS CLOSE TO THE REAL

CONDITIONS WHICH WILL EXIST DURING THE ACTUAL

"QUESTIONING".

DURING YOUR INITIAL CONTACT WITH THE SUBJECT, YOU

SHOULD INFORM HIM AS TO THE ROLE THE INTERPRETER

WILL PLAY DURING THE "QUESTIONING", WHICH IS

SIMPLY TO GIVE AN ACCURATE TRANSLATION OF

EVERYTHING SAID BETWEEN YOU AND THE SUBJECT.

AT THIS TIME, INSTRUCT THE SUBJECT TO SPEAK

DIRECTLY TO YOU — NOT TO THE INTERPRETER, AND

WHILE SPEAKING, TO LOOK DIRECTLY AT YOU — NOT AT

THE INTERPRETER.

INSTRUCT THE SUBJECT TO USE SIMPLE DIRECT

LANGUAGE AND TO AVOID USING PHRASES SUCH AS "TELL

HIM THAT...." OR "I WOULD LIKE TO HAVE YOU SAY

THAT...."

RECORDING AND REPORTING

THE INTERPRETER SHOULD ASSIST YOU IN PREPARING

THE RECORD AND REPORT OF THE "QUESTIONING". THIS

WILL INSURE THAT THERE ARE NO MISUNDERSTANDINGS

OF WHAT THE SUBJECT HAS SAID AND THAT YOU HAVE

ACCURATELY ASSESSED HIS PSYCHOLOGICAL STATE OF

MIND. IF THERE ARE TO BE ADDITIONAL

"QUESTIONING" SESSIONS, YOU CAN NOW PROPERLY

TAILOR YOUR TECHNIQUE TO TAKE ADVANTAGE OF THE

SUBJECT'S PSYCHOLOGICAL STATE.

VI. SUMMARY

REMEMBER, YOUR INTERPRETER CAN SPELL THE DIFFERENCE

BETWEEN SUCCESS AND FAILURE. IF YOU MUST USE AN

INTERPRETER, USE HIM PROPERLY. CONSIDER THE

REQUIREMENTS. TAKE CARE IN SELECTION, TRAIN HIM WELL,

AND USE THE CORRECT TECHNIQUES.

WHEN USING AN INTERPRETER IN A CLASSROOM SITUATION, IF

THERE ARE TWO INSTRUCTORS, THE INTERPRETER MUST WORK

TWICE AS HARD. IF THERE ARE THREE INSTRUCTORS. THE

INTERPRETER MUST WORK THREE TIMES AS HARD.

NO MATTER HOW BADLY THE INSTRUCTOR EXPRESSES HIMSELF.

THE INTERPRETER ALWAYS MAKES HIM SOUND GOOD.

SELECTION OF "QUESTIONERS"

I.   GENERAL.

THE USE OF PROPERLY QUALIFIED AND THOROUGHLY TRAINED
"QUESTIONERS" IS A FUNDAMENTAL REQUIREMENT FOR THE
EFFICIENT EXPLOITATION OF SUBJECTS WHO ARE POTENTIAL
SOURCES OF INTELLIGENCE INFORMATION.

II. QUALIFICATIONS OF CHIEF IMPORTANCE TO A "QUESTIONER"

A.   ENOUGH OPERATIONAL TRAINING AND EXPERIENCE TO

PERMIT QUICK RECOGNITION OF LEADS.

B.   FAMILIARITY WITH THE LANGUAGE TO BE USED.

C.   EXTENSIVE BACKGROUND KNOWLEDGE ABOUT THE

SUBJECT'S NATIVE COUNTRY (AND INTELLIGENCE SERVICE, IF

EMPLOYED BY ONE)

D.   A GENUINE UNDERSTANDING OF THE SOURCE AS A PERSON.

OF THE FOUR TRAITS LISTED, A GENUINE INSIGHT INTO THE

SUBJECT'S CHARACTER AND MOTIVES IS PERHAPS THE MOST

IMPORTANT.

III. PERSONALITY CHARACTERISTICS OF A "QUESTIONER"

THE "QUESTIONER" SHOULD POSSESS SUITABLE PERSONALITY

CHARACTERISTICS WHICH WILL ENABLE HIM TO GAIN THE

COOPERATION OF THE SUBJECT, SOME OF WHICH ARE LISTED

BELOW:

D-5   MOTIVATION: THE DEGREE OF A "QUESTIONER'S" SUCCESS IS DIRECTLY RELATED TO HIS DEGREE OF MOTIVATION. ~~██~~ ~~████████████████~~ HIS MENTAL ATTITUDE TO DO A GOOD JOB IS FELT BY THE SUBJECT AND INCREASES CHANCES OF COOPERATION.

D-6   ALERTNESS: A "QUESTIONER" MUST WATCH FOR ANY INDICATON THAT THE SUBJECT IS WITHHOLDING ADDITIONAL INFORMATION; FOR ANY TENDENCY TO RESIST FURTHER QUESTIONING, FOR DIMINISHING RESISTANCE, FOR CONTRADICTIONS, ETC.

"QUESTIONER" MUST BE CONSTANTLY AWARE OF THE SHIFTING ATTITUDES WHICH NORMALLY CHARACTERIZE A SUBJECT'S REACTION TO "QUESTIONING". HE MUST NOTE THE SUBJECT'S EVERY GESTURE, WORD, AND VOICE INFLECTION AND BE ABLE TO DETERMINE WHY THE SUBJECT IS IN A CERTAIN MOOD OR WHY HIS MOOD SUDDENLY CHANGED. ~~██~~ ~~██~~

D-7   PATIENCE AND TACT: A "QUESTIONER" DISPLAYING PATIENCE AND TACT WILL BE ABLE TO CREATE AND MAINTAIN A FAVORABLE ATMOSPHERE BETWEEN HIMSELF AND THE SUBJECT. THE DISPLAY OF IMPATIENCE WILL ENCOURAGE THE RESISTANT SUBJECT TO REMAIN UNRESPONSIVE EVEN LONGER.

D-8   CREDIBILITY: A "QUESTIONER" MUST MAINTAIN CREDIBILITY WITH THE SUBJECT. FAILURE TO PRODUCE MATERIAL REWARDS WHEN PROMISED MAY ADVERSELY AFFECT FUTURE INTERVIEWS.

D-9   OBJECTIVITY: A "QUESTIONER" MUST HAVE THE ABILITY TO MAINTAIN A DISPASSIONATE MENTAL ATTITUDE REGARDLESS OF THE EMOTIONAL REACTIONS HE MAY ACTUALLY EXPERIENCE OR MAY SIMULATE DURING THE "QUESTIONING".

D-10   SELF CONTROL: A "QUESTIONER" MUST HAVE AN EXCEPTIONAL DEGREE OF SELF CONTROL TO AVOID DISPLAYS OF GENUINE ANGER, IRRITATION, SYMPATHY, OR WEARINESS WHICH MAY CAUSE HIM TO LOSE THE INITIATIVE DURING THE "QUESTIONING".

D-11   ADAPTABILITY: A "QUESTIONER" MUST BE ABLE TO ADAPT HIMSELF TO THE MANY AND VARIED PERSONALITIES WHICH HE MAY ENCOUNTER, TO SMOOTHLY SHIFT HIS TECHNIQUES AND APPROACHES DURING INTERVIEWS. HE MUST ALSO BE ABLE TO ADAPT HIMSELF TO THE OPERATIONAL ENVIRONMENT WHICH OFTEN WILL REQUIRE HIM TO FUNCTION UNDER A VARIETY OF UNFAVORABLE PHYSICAL CONDITIONS.

D-12 PERSERVERANCE: PERSERVERANCE MAKES THE
DIFFERENCE BETWEEN A "QUESTIONER" WHO IS MERELY GOOD
AND ONE WHO IS SUPERIOR. A "QUESTIONER" WHO BECOMES
EASILY DISCOURAGED BY OPPOSITION, NONCOOPERATION, AND
OTHER DIFFICULTIES, WILL NEITHER AGGRESSIVELY PURSUE
THE OBJECTIVE TO A SUCCESSFUL CONCLUSION NOR SEEK
LEADS TO OTHER VALUABLE INFORMATION.

D-13 APPEARANCE AND BEHAVIOR: A NEAT, ORGANIZED, AND
PROFESSIONAL APPEARANCE WILL FAVORABLY INFLUENCE THE
SUBJECT. A FIRM, DELIBERATE, AND BUSINESSLIKE MANNER
OF SPEECH AND ATTITUDE WILL CREATE THE PROPER
ENVIRONMENT FOR A SUCCESSFUL "QUESTIONING". IF A
"QUESTIONER'S" PERSONAL MANNER REFLECTS FAIRNESS,
STRENGTH, AND EFFICIENCY, THE SUBJECT MAY PROVE MORE
COOPERATIVE AND RECEPTIVE TO QUESTIONING.

III. SPECIAL SKILLS AND ABILITIES
A "QUESTIONER" MUST POSSESS, OR ACQUIRE THROUGH
TRAINING AND EXPERIENCE, A NUMBER OF SPECIAL SKILLS
AND KNOWLEDGE.

D-14 A. WRITING AND SPEAKING ABILITY: "QUESTIONING" IS
NOT AN END IN ITSELF. ITS FULL VALUE CAN ONLY BE
REALIZED WITH THE TIMELY DISSEMINATION OF THE
INFORMATION OBTAINED, IN A FORM USABLE TO THE
APPROPRIATE AGENCIES. THEREFORE, A "QUESTIONER" MUST
BE ABLE TO PREPARE AND PRESENT WRITTEN/ORAL REPORTS IN
A CLEAR, COMPLETE, CONCISE, AND ACCURATE MANNER.

D-15   LINGUISTIC SKILL: ALTHOUGH A TRAINED
"QUESTIONER" CAN SUCCESSFULLY WORK THROUGH AN
INTERPRETER. THE RESULTS OBTAINED BY A "QUESTIONER"
WHO IS FLUENT IN THE SUBJECT'S NATIVE LANGUAGE WILL BE
MORE TIMELY AND COMPREHENSIVE. PROFICIENCY IN A
FOREIGN LANGUAGE SHOULD INCLUDE A KNOWLEDGE OF
MILITARY TERMS. IDIOMS. ABBREVIATIONS. SLANG AND LOCAL
DIALECTS.

D-16   C.   SPECIALIZED KNOWLEDGE: THE NATURE OF
EXPLOITATION REQUIRES THAT A "QUESTIONER" HAVE
SPECIALIZED KNOWLEDGE:

D-17   1.   KNOWLEDGE OF THE ORGANIZATION, METHODS OF
OPERATION. AND MISSION OF HIS OWN ESTABLISHMENT
AS WELL AS THOSE OF THE SUBJECT.

D-17   2.   KNOWLEDGE OF THE GEOGRAPHY. HISTORY, AND
CULTURE OF THE AREA IN WHICH HE IS OPERATING AND
OF THE SUBJECT'S HOME COUNTRY. EVEN A RESISTANT
SUBJECT WILL SOMETIMES DISCUSS NON-TACTICAL
TOPICS. AND A KNOWLEDGE OF THE GEOGRAPHY,
ECONOMICS OR POLITICS OF HIS HOME COUNTRY MAY BE
USED TO INDUCE HIM TO TALK. ONCE HE HAS STARTED
TO TALK. THE "QUESTIONER" MAY THEN GRADUALLY
INTRODUCE SIGNIFICANT TOPICS INTO THE DISCUSSION.

D-18   D.   TRAINING IN "QUESTIONING" TECHNIQUES.   THE

EFFECTIVENESS OF A TECHNIQUE DEPENDS ON THE PROPER

SELECTION AND MATCHING OF THE TECHNIQUE TO THE

PERSONALITY OF THE SUBJECT.

D-19   E.   UNDERSTANDING OF BASIC PSYCHOLOGY.   A

"QUESTIONER" CAN BEST ADAPT HIMSELF TO THE PERSONALITY

OF THE SUBJECT IF HE HAS AN UNDERSTANDING OF BASIC

PSYCHOLOGICAL FACTORS. MOTIVATIONS, INHIBITIONS, AND

ATTITUDES.

IV. CONCLUSION

A "QUESTIONER" SHOULD REMEMBER THAT HE AND THE SUBJECT

ARE OFTEN WORKING AT CROSS PURPOSES NOT BECAUSE THE

SUBJECT IS MALEVOLENTLY WITHHOLDING OR MISLEADING BUT

SIMPLY BECAUSE WHAT HE WANTS FROM THE SITUATION IS NOT

WHAT THE "QUESTIONER" WANTS.

A "QUESTIONER'S" GOAL IS TO OBTAIN FACTS CONCERNING

SOMETHING ABOUT WHICH HE FEELS THE SUBJECT HAS

ACQUIRED INFORMATION. BUT THE SUBJECT IS NOT

CONCERNED WITH COMMUNICATING THIS INFORMAION TO HIS

"QUESTIONER"; HE IS CONCERNED WITH "WHAT SORT OF

IMPRESSION AM I MAKING?" AND "WHAT IS GOING TO HAPPEN

TO ME NOW?"

THE SKILLED "QUESTIONER" CAN SAVE A GREAT DEAL OF TIME BY UDERSTANDING THE EMOTIONAL NEEDS OF THE SUBJECT AND RELIEVING THE FEAR WHICH HE FEELS WHEN HE IS SUBJECTED TO "QUESTIONING". SO SIMPLE A MATTER AS GREETING A SUBJECT BY HIS NAME AT THE OPENING OF A SESSION ESTABLISHES IN HIS MIND THE COMFORTING AWARENESS THAT HE IS CONSIDERED AS A PERSON, NOT A SQUEEZABLE SPONGE. WITH THIS UNDERSTANDING ESTABLISHED, THE QUESTIONING CAN MOVE ON TO IMPERSONAL MATTERS AND WILL NOT LATER BE INTERRUPTED BY IRRELEVANT ANSWERS DESIGNED NOT TO PROVIDE FACTS BUT TO PROVE THAT THE SUBJECT IS A RESPECTABLE MEMBER OF THE HUMAN RACE.

ALTHOUGH IT IS OFTEN NECESSARY TO TRICK A SUBJECT INTO TELLING WHAT YOU NEED TO KNOW, ESPECIALLY IN COUNTER INTELLIGENCE "QUESTIONING", THE INITIAL QUESTION WHICH A "QUESTIONER" ASKS HIMSELF SHOULD BE, "HOW CAN I MAKE HIM WANT TO TELL ME WHAT HE KNOWS?" RATHER THAN "HOW CAN I TRAP HIM INTO TELLING WHAT HE KNOWS?"

IF THE SUBJECT IS GENUINELY HOSTILE FOR IDEOLOGICAL REASONS, TECHNIQUES FOR MANIPULATION ARE IN ORDER. BUT THE ASSUMPTION OF HOSTILITY, OR THE USE OF PRESSURE TACTICS AT THE FIRST ENCOUNTER, MAY MAKE A SUBJECT RESISTANT WHO WOULD HAVE RESPONDED TO RECOGNITION OF INDIVIDUALITY AND AN INITIAL ASSUMPTION OF GOOD WILL.

DESIGN AND MANAGEMENT OF A FACILITY

ADMINISTRATIVE/DESIGN CONSIDERATIONS

THE FACILITY SHOULD BE DESIGNED FOR EXPECTED CAPACITY. THE NUMBER OF "QUESTIONING" ROOMS AND DETENTION CELLS REQUIRED IS DIRECTLY PROPORTIONAL TO THE FLOW OF PRISONERS AND THE AVAILABILITY OF "QUESTIONERS". IF POSSIBLE, ALL ACTIVITIES SHOULD BE UNDER ONE ROOF, TO INCLUDE THE FOLLOWING:

E-1   A.   CENTRAL RECEPTION ENTRYWAY FOR ADMITTING ALL PERSONNEL.

E-2   B.   SUPERVISORS' OFFICES.

E-3   C.   OPERATIONS ROOM.

E-4   D.   STAFF OFFICE FOR PLANNING AND REPORTS PREPARATION.

E-5   E.   SLEEPING QUARTERS FOR OFF DUTY GUARDS TO REST.

E-6   F.   FILE ROOM.

E-7   G.   PROCESSING ROOM FOR PRISONERS WITH A STORAGE AREA FOR PERSONAL EFFECTS.

E-8   H.   MEDICAL TREATMENT ROOM WITH A SHOWER FOR EXAMINING AND TREATING PRISONERS.

E-9   I.   KITCHEN FACILITY FOR PREPARING ALL MEALS FOR PRISONERS.

II. SECURITY CONSIDERATIONS

E-10   A.   SHOULD BE CONSTRUCTED IN A REASONABLY SECURE

AREA. SECURE FROM DEMONSTRATIONS, RIOTS, ETC.

E-11   B.   SHOULD NOT BE EASILY OBSERVED FROM OUTSIDE BY

UNAUTHORIZED PERSONNEL.

E-12   C.   SHOULD BE ABLE TO WITHSTAND AN ATTACK.

E-13   BACK-UP UTILITIES, ELECTRICITY, WATER, ETC.

E-14   E.   OVERHEAD AND BUNKER PROTECTION FROM SHELLING.

E-15   BUNKERS OUTSIDE THE FACILITY WITH GOOD FIELDS OF

FIRE.

E-16   G.   FIRING PORTS IN THE OUTSIDE WALL OF THE FACILITY.

E-17   H.   EXTERNAL FENCING OF DENSE MATERIAL TO DETONATE

ROCKETS.

E-18   I.   ENTRY AND EXIT OF ALL PERSONNEL MUST BE STRICTLY

CONTROLLED BY A SYSTEM OF BADGES, WITH PHOTOS,

IDENTIFYING PERSONNEL AND INDICATING AREAS OF ACCESS

(e.g. DIFFERENT COLOR BACKGROUNDS). BADGES NEVER

LEAVE THE FACILITY. THEY ARE PICKED UP AND TURNED AT

RECEPTION.

E-19   J.   VEHICLE ENTRY SHOULD BE LIMITED TO OFFICIAL

VEHICLES AND CONTROLLED BY A DOUBLE GATE BARRIER.

E-20   K.   PARKING AREAS SHOULD BE LOCATED OUTSIDE THE

FACILITY AND AWAY FROM THE OUTSIDE WALL.

III. CELL BLOCK PLANNING

E-21   A.   CELLS SHOULD BE ABOUT 3 METERS LONG AND 2 METERS WIDE.

E-22   B.   CEILING SHOULD BE A MINIMUM OF 3 METERS HIGH WITH SCREENED PROTECTION FOR THE LIGHT.

E-23   C.   CELL DOORS SHOULD BE OF HEAVY STEEL WITH JUDAS PORT FOR VIEWING AND SEPARATE PORT FOR PUTTING FOOD AND WATER INTO THE CELL. (THE SLAMMING OF A HEAVY STEEL DOOR IMPRESSES UPON THE SUBJCT THAT HE IS CUT OFF FROM THE REST OF THE WORLD.)

E-24   D.   WINDOW SHOULD BE SET HIGH IN THE WALL WITH THE CAPABILITY OF BLOCKING OUT LIGHT. (THIS ALLOWS THE "QUESTIONER" TO BE ABLE TO DISRUPT THE SUBJECT'S SENSE OF TIME, DAY AND NIGHT.)

E-25   E.   HEAT, AIR AND LIGHT ~~SHOULD~~ MAY BE EXTERNALLY CONTROLLED, BUT NOT TO THE POINT OF

E-26   F.   BEDDING SHOULD BE MINIMAL — COT AND BLANKET — NO MATTRESS. (THE IDEA IS TO PREVENT THE SUBJECT FROM

E-27   G.   FACILITIES, ~~THE SUBJECT SHOULD HAVE TO ASK TO RELIEVE HIMSELF~~ ~~THEN~~ HE SHOULD EITHER BE GIVEN A BUCKET OR ESCORTED BY A GUARD TO THE LATRINE. THE GUARD STAYS AT HIS SIDE THE ENTIRE TIME HE IS IN THE LATRINE.

E-28   CELLS SHOULD BE SOUNDPROOFED OR INSULATED FROM EACH OTHER.

E-29   I.   THERE SHOULD BE ONE OR TWO PLUSH CELLS FOR COOPERATIVE PRISONERS.

E-30   J.   ONLY AUTHORIZED PERSONS SHOULD BE ALLOWED ACCESS TO THE CELLS.

E-31   K.   THE CELL BLOCK SHOULD HAVE A SECURE TRAVEL ROUTE TO THE "QUESTIONING" ROOMS:

E-32   L.   ONLY ONE SUBJECT SHOULD BE MOVED AT A TIME AND HE SHOULD BE BLINDFOLDED.

E-33   M.   THE HALLWAY OUTSIDE THE CELLS SHOULD HAVE A SERIES OF FLASHING LIGHTS AS A WARNING TO INDICATE WHEN A SUBJECT IS BEING MOVED.

IV.   THE "QUESTIONING" ROOM

THE "QUESTIONING" ROOM IS THE BATTLEFIELD UPON WHICH THE "QUESTIONER" AND THE SUBJECT MEET. HOWEVER, THE "QUESTIONER" HAS THE ADVANTAGE IN THAT HE HAS TOTAL CONTROL OVER THE SUBJECT AND HIS ENVIRONMENT.

ALTHOUGH VARIOUS SITUATIONS MAY REQUIRE SPECIAL EQUIPMENT OR ARRANGEMENTS. HERE IS A BASIC LIST OF DESIRED EQUIPMENT AND A PREFERRED ARRANGEMENT OF THE ROOM AND ITS FURNITURE.

E-34   A.   SHOULD BE AT LEAST 3 X 4 METERS WITH ONLY ONE
ENTRANCE.

E-35   B.   NO WINDOWS, OR WINDOWS THAT CAN BE COMPLETELY
BLACKED OUT.

E-36   C.   SHOULD BE SOUNDPROOFED AND CARPETED.

E-37   D.   SHOULD BE FREE OF DISTRACTIONS, WITH BARE WALLS.
THE SUGGESTED COLOR SCHEME IS AN OFF-WHITE FOR THE
ENTIRE ROOM.

E-38   E.   SHOULD HAVE A WARNING SIGN OR LIGHT OUTSIDE THE
ROOM TO PREVENT INTERRUPTIONS WHEN A "QUESTIONING" IS
BEING CONDUCTED.

E-39   F.   SHOULD HAVE A TWO-WAY MIRROR INSTALLED IN THE
WALL BEHIND THE "QUESTIONER" SO THAT THE SUBJECT'S
REACTIONS CAN BE OBSERVED OR PHOTOGRAPHED; HOWEVER,
CERTAIN PRECAUTIONS MUST BE TAKEN:

        1.   DO NOT PLACE THE MIRROR WHERE THE PRISONER
        CAN OBSERVE HIMSELF, THE ACTIVITIES OF THE
        "QUESTIONER" BEHIND THE DESK, OR SEE THE
        REFLECTION OF THE DOOR.

        2.   THE AREA BEHIND THE MIRROR SHOULD BE AN
        ENCLOSED, DARKENED ROOM, WITH AN INSIDE LATCH ON
        THE DOOR TO PREVENT ENTRY WHILE OBSERVATION IS IN
        PROGRESS.

3.   THE PERSON OBSERVING CANNOT SMOKE, LIGHT A
MATCH OR IN ANY WAY INTRODUCE LIGHT INTO THE
DARKENED ROOM DURING OBSERVATION.

E-40   G.   SHOULD HAVE BUILT-IN RECORDING FACILITIES, WITH A
HIDDEN SWITCH FOR EITHER ACTIVATING THE RECORDER OR
SIGNALING AN ASSISTANT TO DO SO.

1.   THE MICROPHONES SHOULD BE HIDDEN, IN THE
TABLE, WALL. CEILING, ETC.;   BUT, IN ANY
LOCATION. MUST BE ABLE TO GIVE A CLEAR
REPRODUCTION OF THE CONVERSATION.

.2.   THERE SHOULD BE A BACK-UP RECORDER AVAILABLE
IN CASE THE FIRST MALFUNCTIONS.   IT SHOULD BE
LOADED AND READY TO TURN ON WHEN THE FIRST BEGINS
TO RUN OUT OF TAPE.

RECORDING THE "QUESTIONING" PERMITS YOU TO
QUESTION THE SUBJECT WITHOUT HAVING TO TAKE
NOTES. THUS LEAVING THE TABLE BARE IN FRONT OF
HIM WITH NO DISTRACTING PAPERS.

4.   ONCE HE HAS BEGUN TO TALK, YOU DO NOT WANT
TO .BREAK THE RHYTHM OF THE "QUESTIONING".   THE
SIGHT OF YOU WRITING DOWN HIS EVERY WORD CAN
UNNERVE HIM AND MAKE HIM RELUCTANT TO TALK.

5.   REMEMBER, YOU ARE "QUESTIONING" THE SUBJECT
BECAUSE HE IS WITHHOLDING INFORMATION YOU DESIRE,
AND YOU MUST DRAW IT FROM HIM.   THE MICROPHONES
AND RECORDERS ASSIST YOU IN MAINTAINING THE
MOMENTUM AND ATMOSPHERE OF THE "QUESTIONING".

6.   DO NOT ATTEMPT TO RECORD EVERYTHING THAT IS
SAID, ONLY THE CRUCIAL PORTIONS OF THE
"QUESTIONING".   REMEMBER THAT YOU WILL HAVE TO
REVIEW THE TAPES AND THEY MAY HAVE TO BE
TRANSCRIBED AT A LATER DATE.

7.   RECORDINGS ARE AN INVALUABLE AID IN
PREPARING FOR THE NEXT SESSION BECAUSE YOU CAN GO
BACK OVER ANY PORTION OF THE "QUESTIONING" FOR
LEADS OR COMPARE ANSWERS GIVEN AT DIFFERENT
TIMES.   THEY CAN BE PLAYED BACK TO PREVENT DENIAL
OF ADMISSIONS.

8.   TAPES CAN BE EDITED AND SPLICED, WITH
EFFECTIVE RESULTS, IF THE TAMPERING CAN BE KEPT
HIDDEN.   FOR INSTANCE, IT IS MORE EFFECTIVE FOR A
SUBJECT TO HEAR A TAPED CONFESSION OF AN
ACCOMPLICE THAN TO MERELY BE TOLD BY THE
"QUESTIONER" THAT HE HAS CONFESSED.

9. RECORDINGS CAN BE USED BY THE "QUESTIONER" TO STUDY HIS MISTAKES AND HIS MOST EFFECTIVE TECHNIQUES. EXCEPTIONALLY INSTRUCTIVE "QUESTIONINGS" OR PORTIONS THEREOF, CAN BE USED IN THE TRAINING OF OTHERS.

E-41   H. CLOSED CIRCUIT TELEVISION OR A VIDEO TAPE RECORDER IS ANOTHER VALUABLE AID DURING "QUESTIONING". VIDEO TAPES CAN BE REVIEWED TO OBSERVE THE SUBJECT'S REACTIONS TO CERTAIN KEY QUESTIONS. AS WITH TAPE RECORDERS, THERE SHOULD BE A BACK-UP SYSTEM.

E-42   I. THERE SHOULD NOT BE A TELEPHONE IN THE ROOM. IT IS A VISIBLE LINK TO THE OUTSIDE AND ITS PRESENCE MAKES THE SUBJECT FEEL LESS CUT OFF.

ALL CONTROLS FOR LIGHTS, RECORDERS, SIGNALS, ETC. SHOULD BE LOCATED SO THAT YOU CAN EASILY USE THEM WITHOUT ALERTING THE SUBJECT.

NOT EVERY ROOM NEEDS TO BE FULLY EQUIPPED OR IDENTICALLY EQUIPPED.

1. FOR SUBJECTS WHOSE POTENTIAL FOR EXPLOITATION IS NOT VERY HIGH, SIMPLY A ROOM WITH A RECORDER IS SUFFICIENT.

2. AS A HIGHLY PRODUCTIVE SUBJECT BECOMES MORE COOPERATIVE, "QUESTIONING" CAN BE CONTINUED IN A ROOM WHICH HAS A MORE FRIENDLY AND INFORMAL ATMOSPHERE, WITH EASY CHAIRS, CIGARETTES, BEVERAGES, ETC. IN ORDER TO RELAX THE SUBJECT AND INDUCE HIS CONTINUED COOPERATION.

E-43 V. TRAINING OF FACILITY PERSONNEL

ALL PERSONNEL UTILIZED IN THE FACILITY ARE UNDER THE CONTROL OF THE FACILITY CHIEF FOR ADMINISTRATIVE AND LOGISTICAL MATTERS, BUT SHOULD ONLY TAKE ORDERS FROM THE "QUESTIONER" IN MATTERS DEALING WITH THE SUBJECT.

E-43 A. THEY MUST BE THOROUGHLY INDOCTRINATED ON THE INTELLIGENCE ASPECTS OF THEIR JOBS. THE NEED-TO-KNOW PRINCIPLE APPLIES.

E-44 B. THEY MUST UNDERSTAND THE IMPORTANCE OF THEIR PARTICULAR FUNCTION IN THE "QUESTIONING" PROCESS, AND HOW IT CONTRIBUTES TO A SUCCESSFUL EXPLOITATION.

E-45 C. PROCESSING PERSONNEL MUST UNDERSTAND SUBJECT. HANDLING PROCEDURES AND DESIRED RESULTS.

E-46 D. MEDICAL PERSONNEL (YOU MAY WANT TO HAVE THE SUBJECT EXAMINED BY A NURSE).

E-47 E. FILES PERSONNEL ARE TRAINED IN ACCURATELY CHECKING INFORMATION OBTAINED FROM THE SUBJECT AND RELAYING THE RESULTS TO THE "QUESTIONER".

F. EXTERNAL SECURITY PERSONNEL NEED ONLY UNDERSTAND MATTERS DEALING WITH THE PROTECTION OF THE FACILITY AND PREVENTING UNAUTHORIZED ENTRY TO THE FACILITY.

E-48

E-49 G. INTERNAL GUARD PERSONNEL MUST UNDERSTAND WHAT PSYCHOLOGICAL OBJECTIVES THE "QUESTIONER" IS TRYING TO OBTAIN THROUGH THEIR HANDLING OF THE SUBJECT.

E-50 VI. TRAINING OF INTERNAL GUARDS

E-50 A. MUST HAVE UNDERGONE A THOROUGH BACKGROUND

SECURITY CHECK.

E-51 B. MUST BE PROFICIENT IN EMERGENCY PROCEDURES.

E-52 C. MUST UNDERSTAND THE LIMITATIONS ON PHYSICAL CONTACT WITH THE SUBJECT.

E-53 D. MUST UNDERSTAND THE TECHNIQUES USED AND REASONS FOR PSYCHOLOGICAL PREPARATION OF THE SUBJECT.

E-54 E. MUST MOVE SUBJECTS FROM THEIR CELLS TO THE "QUESTIONING" ROOMS WITHOUT ALLOWING THEM TO SEE OR BE SEEN BY OTHER PRISONERS.

THIS SEGREGATION GIVES THE COOPERATIVE SUBJECT A PLAUSIBLE COVER STORY WHEN HE IS LATER MOVED TO ANOTHER COMPOUND WHERE HE MUST LIVE WITH OTHER PRISONERS. NONE OF THEM WILL BE AWARE OF THE LENGTH OF TIME HE WAS QUESTIONED OR WHERE HE WAS DETAINED, AND HE CAN DENY GIVING ANY INFORMATION AT ALL.

F-0

I.   APPREHENSION

F-1   A.   THE MANNER AND TIMING OF ARREST CAN CONTRIBUTE

SUBSTANTIALLY TO THE "QUESTIONER'S" PURPOSE AND SHOULD

BE PLANNED TO ACHIEVE SURPRISE AND THE MAXIMUM AMOUNT

OF MENTAL DISCOMFORT. HE SHOULD THEREFORE BE ARRESTED

AT A MOMENT WHEN HE LEAST EXPECTS IT AND WHEN HIS

MENTAL AND PHYSICAL RESISTANCE IS AT ITS LOWEST.

)-1   THE IDEAL TIME AT WHICH TO MAKE AN ARREST IS IN THE

EARLY HOURS OF THE MORNING. WHEN ARRESTED AT THIS

TIME, MOST SUBJECTS EXPERIENCE INTENSE FEELINGS OF

SHOCK, INSECURITY, AND PSYCHOLOGICAL STRESS AND FOR

THE MOST PART HAVE GREAT DIFFICULTY ADJUSTING TO THE

SITUATION.

F-2   B.   AS TO THE MANNER OF THE ARREST. IT IS VERY

IMPORTANT THAT THE ARRESTING PARTY BEHAVE IN SUCH A

MANNER AS TO IMPRESS THE SUBJECT WITH THEIR

EFFICIENCY. THE SUBJECT SHOULD BE RUDELY AWAKENED AND

IMMEDIATELY BLINDFOLDED AND HANDCUFFED. THE ARRESTING

PARTY SHOULD THEN APPLY THE FOLLOWING PROCEDURE:

C.   SEARCH

SEARCH FOR WEAPONS. EQUIPMENT, OR DOCUMENTS OF

INTELLIGENCE VALUE.   ALL MATERIALS OBTAINED

SHOULD ACCOMPANY THE SUBJECT TO THE "QUESTIONING"

FACILITY.   NO SOUVENIRS!

D.

SILENCE *FROM THE MOMENT OF APPREHENSION TO INITIAL*
------- *QUESTIONING, PRISONERS MAY BE REQUIRED TO*
~~PRISONERS SHOULD~~ MAINTAIN SILENCE AT ALL TIMES,
            AND NOT
~~THEY SHOULD NEVER~~ BE ALLOWED TO SPEAK TO EACH

OTHER.   THE ARRESTING PARTY SHOULD BE INSTRUCTED

TO SPEAK TO THE PRISONERS ONLY AS NECESSARY.

THEY ARE NOT TO "QUESTION" THE PRISONERS. THAT

IS THE JOB OF THE "QUESTIONER".

E.   SEGREGATE
        ----------   *MAY*

PRISONERS ~~SHOULD~~ BE SEGREGATED ~~IMMEDIATELY~~ *AND*

ISOLATION, BOTH PHYSICAL AND PSYCHOLOGICAL. ~~MUST~~ ''

BE MAINTAINED FROM THE MOMENT OF APPREHENSION.

TO INITIAL QUEST . . . , BUT NOT
FOR A PERIOD OF TIME AS EXT . GO A:

F.   SPEED TO THE FACILITY *TO CONSTITUTE TORTURE!*
        -------------------   *DEPT .*

PRISONERS SHOULD BE TRANSPORTED TO THE

"QUESTIONING" FACILITY IN A CLOSED VEHICLE BY WAY

OF A CIRCUITOUS ROUTE TO PREVENT HIS DETECTING

WHERE HE IS BEING HELD.

G.   THE ARRESTING PARTY SHOULD USE ONLY SUFFICIENT

- FORCE TO EFFECT THE ARREST.   NO VIOLENCE!   IF THEY

BREAK THE SUBJECT'S JAW,. HE WILL NOT BE ABLE TO ANSI ''

QUESTIONS DURING THE "QUESTIONING".

F-8   H.   A "QUESTIONER" SHOULD NOT PARTICIPATE IN THE

ARREST BECAUSE THE SUBJECT WILL REACT TO HIM QUITE

DIFFERENTLY IF HE HAS NEVER SEEN HIM BEFORE.   A

"QUESTIONER" SHOULD RECIEVE A COMPLETE REPORT FROM THE

CHIEF OF THE ARRESTING PARTY WHICH SHOULD INCLUDE A

DESCRIPTION OF CIRCUMSTANCES DURING THE ARREST, A LIST

OF ITEMS TAKEN FROM THE SUBJECT, AND ANY STATEMENTS

MADE BY THE SUBJECT.

II.   HANDLING UPON ARRIVAL AT THE FACILITY

F-9   A.   SUBJECT IS BROUGHT INTO THE FACILITY BLINDFOLDED

AND HANDCUFFED AND SHOULD REMAIN SO DURING THE ENTIRE

PROCESSING.

F-10   B.   ANY TIME THE SUBJECT IS MOVED FOR ANY REASON, HE

SHOULD BE BLINDFOLDED AND HANDCUFFED.

F-11   C.   SUBJECT SHOULD BE REQUIRED TO COMPLY IMMEDIATELY

AND PRECISELY WITH ALL INSTRUCTIONS.

F-12   D.   ALL ITEMS BELONGING TO THE SUBJECT ARE

INVENTORIED AND STORED, WITH A COPY OF THE LIST GOING

TO THE "QUESTIONER".

F-13   E.   SUBJECT IS FINGERPRINTED AND PHOTOGRAPHED, USING

CAUTION WHEN REMOVING BLINDFOLD.

F-14   F.   SUBJECT IS COMPLETELY STRIPPED AND TOLD TO TAKE A

SHOWER.   BLINDFOLD REMAINS IN PLACE WHILE SHOWERING

AND GUARD WATCHES THROUGHOUT.

F-14   SUBJECT IS GIVEN A THOROUGH MEDICAL EXAMINATION.

INCLUDING ALL BODY CAVITIES. BY THE FACILITY DOCTOR OR

NURSE.

F-15   SUBJECT IS PROVIDED WITH ILL-FITTING CLOTHING

(FAMILIAR CLOTHING REINFORCES IDENTITY AND THUS THE

CAPACITY FOR RESISTANCE).

F-16.   I.   SUBJECT IS THEN TAKEN TO AN INDIVIDUAL CELL WHERE

THE BLINDFOLD AND HANDCUFFS ARE REMOVED AFTER HE

ENTERS THE CELL.

F-17   J. SUBJECT IS NOT PERMITTED READING MATTER OF ANY

KIND.

F-18   K.   TOTAL ISOLATION SHOULD BE MAINTAINED UNTIL AFTER

THE FIRST "QUESTIONING" SESSION.   CONDITIONS CAN BE

ADJUSTED AFTER THIS SESSION.

F-19   L.   SUBJECT SHOULD BE MADE TO BELIEVE THAT HE HAS

BEEN FORSAKEN BY HIS COMRADES.

F-20   M.   THROUGHOUT HIS DETENTION, SUBJECT MUST BE

CONVINCED THAT HIS "QUESTIONER" CONTROLS HIS ULTIMATE

DESTINY, AND THAT HIS ABSOLUTE COOPERATION IS

ESSENTIAL TO SURVIVAL.

SCREENING OF SUBJECTS
                        =========---=========

        I.   GENERAL

G-1   A.   SCREENING IS THE PROCESS OF OBTAINING BACKGROUND

        BIOGRAPHICAL AND PSYCHOLOGICAL DATA FROM SUBJECTS IN

        ORDER TO DETERMINE FUTURE HANDLING.   FOR EXAMPLE,

        CUSTOMS SCREENS TRAVELERS TO IDENTIFY SUSPECTS WHO FIT

        THE PSYCHOLOGICAL PROFILE OF A SMUGGLER.   THOSE WHO

        DO   ARE THEN DETAINED FOR FURTHER QUESTIONING AND

        SEARCHING.

        THE SCREENING OF LARGE GROUPS OF PRISONERS SUCH AS

        P.O.W.'s OR REFUGEES PRIOR TO "QUESTIONING" HAS A

        SIMILAR PURPOSE.   ONLY SUBJECTS WITH KNOWLEDGE OF

        POTENTIAL INTELLIGENCE VALUE SHOULD BE SELECTED FOR

        "QUESTIONING".

G-2   B.   THE SCREENER SHOULD CONSIDER THE FOLLOWING

        FACTORS WHEN MAKING SELECTIONS:

                1.   OVERALL INTELLIGENCE REQUIREMENTS AND

                PRIORITIES.

                2.   HOUSING CAPACITY AND NUMBER OF "QUESTIONERS"

                AVAILABLE.

                3.   ESTIMATED INTELLIGENCE POTENTIAL OF THE

                SUBJECT.

THE FOLLOWING GUIDELINES WILL AID THE SCREENER IN
ESTABLISHING THE PRIORITY AND POTENTIAL OF A SUBJECT:

G-3   C.   PRIORITY "A" - SUBJECTS WHO ARE MOST LIKELY TO
-physicists   HAVE: TECHNICAL OR SCIENTIFIC KNOWLEDGE OF
-chemists   INTELLIGENCE VALUE, NAMES OF OFFICERS AND AGENTS
-satellites   WORKING FOR THE OPPOSITION, DIRECT INVOLVEMENT IN
- etc. etc.   SUBVERSIVE ACTS.

G-4   PRIORITY "B" - SUBJECTS WHO HAVE OTHER
                 INFORMATION OF INTELLIGENCE VALUE ON A SUBJECT
                 THAT WARRANTS "QUESTIONING", SUCH AS INFORMATION
                 OF IMMEDIATE TACTICAL VALUE.

                 PRIORITY "C" - SUBJECTS WHO HAVE INFORMATION
G-5   WHICH CAN BE USED TO VERIFY OR CORROBORATE OTHER
                 INFORMATION.

G-6   PRIORITY "D" - SUBJECTS WHO HAVE NO INFORMATION
                 OF INTELLIGENCE VALUE.

          D.   SCREENING SHOULD BE CONDUCTED BY SOMEONE OTHER
          THAN THE "QUESTIONER" BECAUSE THERE IS AN IMPORTANT
          DIFFERENCE IN WHAT THE TWO ARE TRYING TO OBTAIN. THE
          SCREENER WANTS TO OBTAIN PERSONAL INFORMATION ABOUT
          THE SUBJECT HIMSELF. THE "QUESTIONER" WANTS TO OBTAIN
          INFORMATION TO SATISFY SPECIFIC REQUIREMENTS.

E.   THE TASK OF SCREENING IS MADE EASIER BY THE FACT
THAT THE SCREENER IS INTERESTED IN THE SUBJECT.   MOST
SUBJECTS WILL SPEAK WITH SOME FREEDOM ABOUT CHILDHOOD
EVENTS AND FAMILIAL RELATIONSHIPS.   EVEN A PROVOCATEUR
WHO IS TRAINED TO RECITE A COVER STORY AND SUBSTITUTES
A FICTICIOUS PERSON FOR HIS FATHER WILL DISCLOSE SOME
OF HIS FEELINGS ABOUT HIS REAL FATHER.

F.   IF THE SCREENER CAN PUT THE SUBJECT AT EASE, HE
IS UNLIKELY TO FEEL THAT A CASUAL CONVERSATION ABOUT
HIMSELF IS DANGEROUS.   FOR EXAMPLE, ROUTINE QUESTIONS
ABOUT SCHOOL TEACHERS, EMPLOYERS, OR GROUP LEADERS
WILL LEAD THE SUBJECT TO REVEAL HOW HE FEELS ABOUT HIS
PARENTS, SUPERIORS, AND OTHERS OF EMOTIONAL
CONSEQUENCE TO HIM BECAUSE OF ASSOCIATIVE LINKS IN HIS
MIND.

G-7   II.   INTELLIGENCE CATEGORIES
THE FOLLOWING CATEGORIES ARE EXAMPLES OF TYPES OF
SUBJECTS WHO MOST FREQUENTLY PROVIDE INFORMATION OF
INTELLIGENCE VALUE:

G-7   A.   TRAVELLERS
ARE USUALLY INTERVIEWED, DEBRIEFED, OR QUESTIONED
THROUGH TECHNIQUES OF ELICITATION.   THEY ARE ONLY
"QUESTIONED", IF THEY ALSO FALL INTO ONE OF THE
OTHER CATEGORIES.

Why do these return.
 - love of country // family
 - trained by Soviets??

G-8   B.   REPATRIATES

                 SOMETIMES "QUESTIONED". BUT OTHER TECHNIQUES USED

                 MORE OFTEN.

G-9   DEFECTORS. ESCAPEES AND REFUGEES

                 ARE NORMALLY "QUESTIONED" SUFFICIENTLY TO TEST

                 BONA FIDES. HOWEVER, REMEMBER THAT BONA FIDES

                 CANNOT BE ESTABLISHED CONCLUSIVELY BY

                 "QUESTIONING" ALONE. EXPERIENCE HAS SHOWN THAT

                 THE OPPOSITION IS WELL AWARE OF THIS CHANNEL AS A

                 MEANS OF PLANTING THEIR AGENTS IN TARGET

                 COUNTRIES.

G-10   D.   AGENTS

                 ARE MORE FREQUENTLY DEBRIEFED THAN "QUESTIONED".

                 IF IT IS ESTABLISHED THAT AN AGENT BELONGS TO ONE

                 OF THE NEXT THREE CATEGORIES. THEN HE IS

                 "QUESTIONED".

G-11   E.   PROVOCATEURS

                 USUALLY POSE AS DEFECTORS, ESCAPEES, OR-REFUGEES

                 IN ORDER TO PENETRATE EMIGRE GROUPS. AN

                 INTELLIGENCE SERVICE. OR OTHER TARGETS ASSIGNED

                 BY THE OPPOSITION. THEY ARE TRAINED IN DECEPTION

                 AND THE USE OF A COVER STORY. DETECTION OF A

                 PROVOCATEUR REQUIRES SKILLED "QUESTIONING".

G-12   F.   DOUBLE AGENTS

FREQUENTLY ARE NOT "QUESTIONED" UNLESS IT IS

DETERMINED THAT THEY ARE GIVING THE EDGE TO THE

OPPOSITION.

G-13   G.   FABRICATORS

ARE USUALLY "QUESTIONED" FOR PREVENTIVE REASONS,

TO NULLIFY ANY DAMAGE TO YOUR SERVICE.

FABRICATORS HAVE LITTLE INTELLIGENCE SIGNIFICANCE

BUT ARE NOTORIOUSLY SKILLFUL TIMEWASTERS. THE

PROFESSIONAL PEDDLER WITH SEVERAL INTELLIGENCE

SERVICE CONTACTS MAY BE AN EXCEPTION, BUT HE WILL

USUALLY GIVE THE EDGE TO A HOST SECURITY SERVICE

BECAUSE OTHERWISE HE CANNOT FUNCTION..WITH

IMPUNITY.

G-14   III. PERSONALITY CATEGORIES

A.   THE SCREENING OF INDIVIDUALS PRIOR TO

"QUESTIONING" CAN PROVIDE A "QUESTIONER" WITH

BACKGROUND DATA WHICH WILL GIVE HIM PSYCHOLOGICAL

INSIGHT TO THE SUBJECT. THIS PRELIMINARY

PSYCHOLOGICAL ASSESSMENT WILL PERMIT HIM TO SELECT

"QUESTIONING" TECHNIQUES MATCHED TO THE PERSONALITY OF

THE SUBJECT.

B.   A REAL UNDERSTANDING OF THE SUBJECT IS WORTH FAR
MORE THAN A THOROUGH KNOWLEDGE OF THIS OR THAT
CATEGORY TO WHICH HE HAS BEEN ASSIGNED.   FOR   .
"QUESTIONING" PURPOSES THE WAYS IN WHICH HE DIFFERS
FROM THE ABSTRACT CATEGORY MAY BE MORE SIGNIFICANT
THAN THE WAYS IN WHICH HE CONFORMS.   HOWEVER, THE
SCREENER DOES NOT HAVE TIME TO PROBE THE DEPTHS OF
EACH SUBJECT'S INDIVIDUALITY AND MUST THEREFORE MAKE
USE OF CATEGORIZING.

C.   A "QUESTIONER" MUST NOT MAKE THE MISTAKE OF
ASSUMING THAT BECAUSE A SUBJECT HAS ONE OR TWO
CHARACTERISTICS OF A CATEGORY, THAT HE AUTOMATICALLY
BELONGS IN THAT CATEGORY.   MOST SUBJECTS WILL SHOW
CHARACTERISTICS OF MORE THAN ONE CATEGORY, SOME WILL
NOT FIT INTO ANY OF THE CATEGORIES.

D.   WITH THESE RESERVATIONS IN MIND, THE FOLLOWING
NINE PSYCHOLOGICAL/EMOTIONAL CATEGORIES ARE DESCRIBED.
THEY ARE BASED UPON THE ASSUMPTION THAT A SUBJECT'S
PAST IS ALWAYS REFLECTED IN HIS PRESENT ETHICS AND
BEHAVIOR AND THAT ALL INDIVIDUALS, REGARDLESS OF
CULTURAL AND GEOGRAPHIC BACKGROUNDS, WILL REACT IN
ESSENTIALLY THE SAME WAY TO THE SAME TECHNIQUES.

G-14 ✳   THE ORDERLY-OBSTINATE SUBJECT.

G-15   - THE SUBJECT IN THIS CATEGORY IS OFTEN INTELLECTUAL.

G-15   - HE TENDS TO THINK LOGICALLY AND ACT DELIBERATELY.

G-16   HE IS PUNCTUAL, ORDERLY, TIDY

G-17   - HE IS FRUGAL, NOT IMPULSIVE

G-18   - HE IS VINDICTIVE OR VENGEFUL

G-18   HE IS STUBBORN

G-20   - HE IS SECRETIVE, DISINCLINED TO CONFIDE IN OTHERS.

G-21   - HE CONSIDERS HIMSELF SUPERIOR TO OTHER PEOPLE.

G-22   - HE SOMETIMES HAS HIS OWN SYSTEM OF MORALITY.

G-23   HE AVOIDS ANY REAL COMMITMENT TO ANYTHING.

G-24   - HE IS INTENSELY CONCERNED ABOUT PERSONAL

          POSSESSIONS, OFTEN CARRYING SHINY COINS, KEEPSAKES, OR

          OTHER OBJECTS HAVING SYMBOLIC VALUE.

   G-25   - HE USUALLY HAS A HISTORY OF ACTIVE REBELLION IN

          CHILDHOOD.

G-27   - HE HAS DEVELOPED A PROFOUND FEAR AND HATRED OF

          AUTHORITY.
          ✳

          WHEN DEALING WITH AN ORDERLY-OBSTINATE SUBJECT:

G-27   - AVOID THE ROLE OF HOSTILE AUTHORITY.

G-28   - THREATS AND THREATENING GESTURES, TABLE POUNDING,

G-29   POUNCING ON EVASIONS AND LIES, OR ANY SIMILAR

          AUTHORITATIVE TACTICS WILL ONLY AWAKEN OLD ANXIETIES

          AND HABITUAL DEFENSE MECHANISMS.

G-30   - TO ATTAIN RAPPORT, BE FRIENDLY.

G-31   - THE ROOM AND "QUESTIONER" SHOULD LOOK EXCEPTIONALLY

          NEAT.

G-32	THE OPTIMISTIC SUBJECT

G-33	- THIS TYPE OF SUBJECT IS ALMOST CONSTANTLY
	HAPPY-GO-LUCKY. HE SEEMS TO ENJOY A CONTINUAL STATE
	OF WELL-BEING.
G-34	- HE IS IMPULSIVE, INCONSISTENT, AND UNDEPENDABLE.
G-35	- HE IS NOT ABLE TO WITHSTAND VERY MUCH PRESSURE.
G-36	- HE REACTS TO A CHALLENGE BY RUNNING AWAY TO AVOID
	CONFLICT.
G-37	- HE IS OFTEN THE YOUNGEST MEMBER OF A LARGE FAMILY.
G-38	- HE HAS USUALLY HAD A GREAT DEAL OF OVER INDULGENCE
	IN EARLY CHILDHOOD.

WHEN DEALING WITH AN OPTIMISTIC SUBJECT:

G-40

G-39	- AVOID PRESSURE TACTICS OR HOSTILITY WHICH WILL MAKE
G-40	HIM RETREAT INSIDE HIMSELF
G-41	- REASSURANCE WILL BRING HIM OUT. THE OPTIMISTIC
	SUBJECT RESPONDS BEST TO A KINDLY, PARENTAL APPROACH.
G-42	- HE CAN OFTEN BE HANDLED EFFECTIVELY BY THE "FRIEND
	AND FOE" TECHNIQUE DISCUSSED LATER.

G-43   THE GREEDY, DEMANDING SUBJECT
--- --------------------

G-44   - THIS TYPE OF SUBJECT IS EXTREMELY DEPENDENT AND

PASSIVE.

G-45   HE CONSTANTLY DEMANDS THAT OTHERS TAKE CARE OF HIM.

G-46   - HE TRIES TO PERSUADE OTHERS TO DEFEND HIM SAYING,

"LET'S YOU AND HIM FIGHT."

G-47   - HE IS LIKELY TO SHIFT LOYALTIES IF HE FEELS HIS

SPONSOR HAS LET HIM DOWN. AN EXAMPLE IS A DEFECTOR

WHO FEELS HIS DESIRES WERE NOT SATISFIED IN HIS HOME

COUNTRY.

G-48   - HE IS SUBJECT TO FREQUENT DEPRESSIONS AND MAY EVEN

TRY TO COMMIT SUICIDE.

G-49   - HE USUALLY SUFFERED FROM DEPRIVATION OF AFFECTION OR

SECURITY IN EARLY CHILDHOOD.

WHEN DEALING WITH A GREEDY, DEMANDING SUBJECT:

G-50   - BE CAREFUL NOT TO REBUFF HIM; OTHERWISE RAPPORT WILL

BE DESTROYED.

G-51   - DO NOT ACCEDE TO DEMANDS WHICH CANNOT BE MET.

GRANTING AN UNIMPORTANT FAVOR MAY SATISFY HIM. BECAUSE

HIS DEMANDS ARISE NOT FROM A SPECIFIC NEED BUT AS AN

EXPRESSION OF HIS NEED FOR SECURITY.

G-52   - ANY MANIFESTATION OF CONCERN FOR HIS WELL-BEING WILL

BE REASSURING TO HIM.

G-53   - ADOPTING THE TONE OF AN UNDERSTANDING FATHER OR BIG

BROTHER IS LIKELY TO MAKE HIM RESPONSIVE.

* always wants more;
* hold of it -- so carrot & stick
  . . :

G-54   THE ANXIOUS. SELF-CENTERED SUBJECT

G-55   THIS TYPE OF SUBJECT IS UNUSUALLY FEARFUL.

G-56   - HE IS ENGAGED IN A CONSTANT STRUGGLE TO CONCEAL HIS

        FEARS.

G-57   - HE IS FREQUENTLY A DAREDEVIL PRETENDING THERE IS NO

        SUCH THING AS DANGER.

G-58   - HE TENDS TO BRAG AND OFTEN LIES OUT OF A DESIRE FOR

        APPROVAL OR PRAISE.

        - HE MAY HAVE BEEN DECORATED FOR BRAVERY AS A SOLDIER,

        HAVING EXPOSED HIMSELF TO DANGER ONLY IN ANTICIPATION

        OF REWARDS AND APPROVAL.

G-59   - HE IS INTENSELY VAIN AND SENSITIVE.

        THE CONCEALED ANXIETY OF THIS SUBJECT PROVIDES THE

        OPPORTUNITY FOR MANIPULATION. HIS DESIRE TO IMPRESS

        WILL BE QUICKLY EVIDENT. HE IS LIKELY TO BE TALKATIVE.

G-60   - IGNORING OR RIDICULING HIS BRAGGING. OR CUTTING HIM

G-61   SHORT IS LIKELY TO MAKE HIM RESENTFUL.

G-62   TAKE ADVANTAGE OF HIS DESIRE TO IMPRESS.

G-63   - PLAYING UPON HIS VANITY OR PRAISING HIS COURAGE IS

        LIKELY TO BE SUCCESSFUL.

G-64 THE GUILT-RIDDEN SUBJECT

G-65 - THIS TYPE OF SUBJECT HAS A STRONG, CRUEL,

      UNREALISTIC CONSCIENCE.

G-66 - HE OFTEN ATTEMPTS TO PROVE HE HAS BEEN TREATED

      UNJUSTLY.

G-67 - HE MAY HAVE BEEN FREQUENTLY SCOLDED OR PUNISHED AS A

      CHILD, OR MAY HAVE BEEN A "MODEL" CHILD WHO REPRESSED

      ALL NATURAL HOSTILITIES.

G-68 - HE MAY PROVOKE UNJUST TREATMENT TO ASSUAGE HIS

      CONSCIENCE THROUGH PUNISHMENT.

G-69 - HE MAY FALSELY CONFESS TO CRIMES.

G-70 - HE MAY COMMIT CRIMES IN ORDER TO CONFESS AND BE

      PUNISHED.

G-71   MASOCHISTS BELONG IN THIS CATEGORY.

      - COMPULSIVE GAMBLERS WHO FIND NO PLEASURE IN WINNING

      BUT FIND RELIEF IN LOSING BELONG IN THIS CATEGORY.

                                    DIFFICULT
      THE GUILT-RIDDEN SUBJECT IS ∧ TO "QUESTION".

G-72 - AVOID ACCUSATIONS WHICH MAY TRIGGER FALSE

      CONFESSIONS TO HOSTILE CLANDESTINE ACTIVITY IN WHICH

      HE WAS NOT INVOLVED.

G-73 - IF PUNISHED, HE MAY REMAIN SILENT, ENJOYING THE

      "PUNISHMENT".

G-74 - SUBJECTS WITH INTENSE GUILT FEELINGS MAY CEASE

      RESISTANCE AND COOPERATE IF PUNISHED IN SOME WAY,

      BECAUSE OF THE GRATIFICATION INDUCED BY PUNISHMENT.

G-75 THE SUBJECT WRECKED BY SUCCESS

G-76   THIS TYPE OF SUBJECT CANNOT TOLERATE SUCCESS.

G-77   HE HAS A CONSCIENCE WHICH FORBIDS THE PLEASURES OF

ACCOMPLISHMENT AND RECOGNITION. HE ENJOYS HIS

AMBITIONS ONLY AS LONG AS THEY REMAIN FANTASIES.

G-78   - HE GOES THROUGH LIFE FAILING AT CRITICAL POINTS. HE

HAS A HISTORY OF ALMOST COMPLETING A SIGNIFICANT

ASSIGNMENT BUT SOMETHING ALWAYS INTERVENES. THIS

"SOMETHING" IS ACTUALLY A SENSE OF GUILT OF THE KIND

DESCRIBED IN THE LAST CATEGORY.

G-79   - HE FREQUENTLY PROJECTS HIS GUILT FEELINGS AND BLAMES

ALL HIS FAILURES ON SOMEONE ELSE.

G-80   - HE HAS A STRONG NEED TO SUFFER AND MAY SEEK DANGER

OR INJURY.

G-81   - HE IS OFTEN ACCIDENT PRONE

WHEN DEALING WITH THE SUBJECT WRECKED BY SUCCESS:

G-82   - AVOID QUESTIONING WHICH IMPINGES UPON HIS FEELINGS

G-83   OF GUILT OR THE REASONS FOR HIS PAST FAILURES. THIS

WILL ONLY RESULT IN SUBJECTIVE DISTORTIONS. THE

SUCCESSFUL "QUESTIONER" WILL ISOLATE THIS AREA OF

UNRELIABILITY.

G-84 THE SCHIZOID SUBJECT

G-85 - THIS SUBJECT LIVES IN A FANTASY WORLD MOST OF THE

TIME.

G-86 HE OFTEN CANNOT DISTINGUISH FANTASY FROM REALITY.

G-87 TO HIM, THE REAL WORLD SEEMS EMPTY AND MEANINGLESS.

G-88 - HE IS EXTREMELY INTOLERANT OF ANY FRUSTATION THAT

OCCURS IN THE REAL WORLD AND DEALS. WITH IT BY

WITHDRAWING INTO HIS FANTASY WORLD.

G-89 - HE HAS NO REAL ATTACHMENTS TO OTHERS.

G-90 - ANY LINK TO A GROUP OR COUNTRY WILL ONLY BE

TRANSITORY.

G-91 - ALTHOUGH HE RETREATS FROM REALITY, HE DOES NOT WANT

TO FEEL ABANDONED.

G-92 - HE NEEDS EXTERNAL APPROVAL.

G-93 - HE IS LIKELY TO LIE READILY TO WIN APPROVAL. BUT

BECAUSE HE IS NOT ALWAYS CAPABLE OF DISTINGUISHING

BETWEEN FACT AND FANTASY, HE MAY BE UNAWARE OF LYING.

THE SCHIZOID SUBJECT'S DESIRE FOR APPROVAL PROVIDES

THE "QUESTIONER" WITH A HANDLE.

G-93 - AVOID ACCUSATIONS OF LYING OR OTHER INDICATIONS OF

G-94 DISESTEEM WHICH MAY PROVOKE WITHDRAWAL FROM THE

SITUATION.

G-95 - THE TRUTH CAN BE TEASED OUT OF THE SCHIZOID IF HE IS

- CONVINCED THAT HE WILL NOT INCUR FAVOR BY LYING OR

DISFAVOR BY TELLING THE TRUTH.

G-96   - THE EXCEPTION

G-97   - THIS TYPE OF SUBJECT FEELS THAT THE WORLD OWES HIM A GREAT DEAL.

G-98   - HE FEELS THAT HE HAS SUFFERED A GROSS MISFORTUNE SUCH AS A PHYSICAL DEFORMITY, EARLY LOSS OF A PARENT. OR PAINFUL ILLNESS AS A CHILD.

G-99   - HE REGARDS THIS MISFORTUNE AS AN INJUSTICE WHICH MUST BE RECTIFIED.

G-100   - HE CLAIMS AS HIS RIGHT, PRIVILEGES NOT PERMITTED OTHERS.

G-101   - IF THE CLAIM IS IGNORED OR DENIED, HE MAY BECOME REBELLIOUS.

G-102   - HE IS LIKELY TO MAKE DEMANDS FOR MONEY, AID, AND OTHER FAVORS THAT ARE COMPLETELY OUT OF PROPORTION TO THE VALUE OF HIS INFORMATION.

THE EXCEPTION IS BEST HANDLED BY:

G-103 — LISTENING TO HIS GRIEVANCES (WITHIN REASONABLE TIMELIMITS).

G-104 — AVOIDING ANY AMBIGOUS REPLIES TO DEMANDS WHICH MIGHT BE INTERPRETED AS ACQUIESCENCE.

G-105 — MAKING NO COMMITMENTS THAT CANNOT BE DISCHARGED FULLY.

G-106 — DEFECTORS FROM OTHER INTELLIGENCE SERVICES, DOUBLE AGENTS, AND PROVOCATEURS, IF THEY BELONG TO THIS

G-106 CATEGORY, ARE VERY RESPONSIVE TO SUGGESTIONS FROM THE "QUESTIONER" THAT THEY HAVE BEEN TREATED UNFAIRLY BY THE OTHER SERVICE.

G-107 — REMEMBER THAT HE HAS NO SENSE OF LOYALTY. IF HE FEELS WRONGED BY YOUR SERVICE, HE IS VERY LIKELY TO GO TO THE NEWSPAPERS OR COURTS. THIS SHOULD BE TAKEN INTO ACCOUNT BEFORE ANY PLANNED OPERATIONAL USE.

G-108   THE AVERAGE OR NORMAL SUBJECT

G-109   - MAY EXHIBIT MOST OR ALL OF THE CHARACTERISTICS OF

         THE OTHER CATEGORIES FROM TIME TO TIME.

G-110   - BUT NONE OF THEM IS PERSISTENTLY DOMINANT. THE

         AVERAGE SUBJECT'S QUALITIES OF OBSTINACY, OPTIMISM,

         ANXIETY, ETC. ARE NOT OVERRIDING EXCEPT FOR SHORT

         PERIODS OF TIME.

G-111   - HIS REACTIONS TO THE WORLD AROUND HIM RESULT FROM

         EVENTS IN THAT WORLD AND ARE NOT THE PRODUCT OF RIGID,

         SUBJECTIVE PATTERNS AS IS TRUE WITH THE OTHER

         CATEGORIES DISCUSSED.

PLANNING THE "QUESTIONING"

H-1 I.   REASONS FOR A PLAN

A.   NO TWO "QUESTIONINGS" ARE THE SAME.   EACH IS
SHAPED DEFINITIVELY BY THE PERSONALITY OF THE SUBJECT.
ONLY WHEN THE STRENGTHS AND WEAKNESSES OF THE SUBJECT
HAVE BEEN IDENTIFIED AND UDERSTOOD DOES IT BECOME
POSSIBLE TO PLAN REALISTICALLY.

H-2   B.   THE LONG RANGE GOAL OF THE "QUESTIONING" IS TO
OBTAIN FROM THE SUBJECT ALL USEFUL INFORMATION THAT HE

H-3   HAS.   TO ACHIEVE THIS. HIS CAPACITY FOR RESISTANCE
SHOULD

H-4   ~~MUST~~ BE ~~DESTROYED~~ ~~AND~~ REPLACED WITH A COOPERATIVE
ATTITUDE.

H-5   C.   "QUESTIONING" IS AN ONGOING INTERPERSONAL PROCESS
AND EVERYTHING THAT TAKES PLACE INFLUENCES ALL
SUBSEQUENT EVENTS.   CONTINUAL APPLICATION OF
TECHNIQUES THAT FAIL ONLY BOLSTER THE SUBJECT'S
CONFIDENCE AND HIS ABILITY TO RESIST.   THEREFORE, IT
IS WRONG TO TRY ONE TECHNIQUE AFTER ANOTHER UNTIL THE
PROPER METHOD IS DISCOVERED BY CHANCE.   ·THIS TYPE OF
AIMLESS APPROACH CAN RUIN THE CHANCE FOR SUCCESS EVEN
IF PROPERLY PLANNED TECHNIQUES ARE USED LATER.

II.- STEPS PRIOR TO CONSTRUCTION OF THE PLAN

H-6   A.   THE SUBJECT IS SCREENED TO DETERMINE:

H-7   1.   HIS BACKGROUND BIOGRAPHIC DATA WHICH IS USED

TO CONDUCT TRACES AND VERIFY FILES HOLDINGS.

2.   HIS KNOWLEDGEABILITY IN RELATION TO

REQUIREMENTS.

3.   HIS PREVIOUS EXPOSURE TO "QUESTIONING" OR

DETENTION.

H-8   B.   A PSYCHOLOGICAL ASSESSMENT IS MADE TO DETERMINE:

H-9   1.   INTO WHICH EMOTIONAL CATEGORY HE FITS.

2.   ANY PSYCHOLOGICAL ABNORMALITIES.

3.   HIS DEGREE OF WILLINGNESS TO COOPERATE.

4.   WHAT HIS POTENTIAL VULNERABILITIES ARE.

5.   HOW HE VIEWS HIS POTENTIAL FOR SURVIVING HIS

SITUATION.

6.   WHETHER HE FEELS THAT REVEALING THE DESIRED

INFORMATION POSES A PERSONAL THREAT TO HIM.

7.   WHAT COURSE OF ACTION WILL REDUCE HIS

ABILITY TO RESIST.

H-10   C.   DETAILED STUDY OF THE SUBJECT'S ORGANIZATION.

H-11   D.   STUDY THE AREAS IN WHICH HE HAS OPERATED.

H-12   E.   REVIEW ALL RECENT TRAVEL OF THE SUBJECT.

H-13   F.   STUDY THE SUBJECT'S PERSONAL BELONGINGS.

H-14   G.   REVIEW RELATED INFORMATION OBTAINED FROM OTHER

SOURCES.

H-15   H.   WITHIN SECURITY LIMITATIONS, CIRCULATE THE
SUBJECT'S BIO-DATA TO OTHER INTERESTED AGENCIES WITH A
REQUEST FOR TAILORED REQUIREMENTS.

H-16   I.   COLLATE ALL OF THE ABOVE.

III.   SPECIFIC DETAILS TO BE INCLUDED IN THE PLAN
THE PLAN SHOULD PREPARED SYSTEMATICALLY, BUT ALWAYS
ALLOW FOR REVISION AS THE "QUESTIONING" PROGRESSES.
THE PSYCHOLOGICAL ASSESSMENT IS A CONTINUING PROCESS
AND MUST BE MODIFIED PERIODICALLY BASED UPON NEW
EVALUATIONS.

H-17   A.   OBJECTIVE OF THE "QUESTIONING"

H-18   1.   WHAT INFORMATION DO WE WANT TO OBTAIN?

H-18   WHY DO WE FEEL THE SUBJECT HAS THIS
INFORMATION?

H-18   -.   HOW IMPORTANT IS THIS INFORMATION?

H-18   4.   HOW CAN THIS INFORMATION BE BEST OBTAINED?

H-18   IF SPECIFIC GOALS CANNOT BE DISCERNED
CLEARLY, FURTHER INVESTIGATION IS NEEDED BEFORE
THE "QUESTIONING" STARTS.

H-18   6.   ANY CONFUSION CONCERNING THE PURPOSE OF THE
"QUESTIONING" OR THE BELIEF THAT THE PURPOSE WILL
TAKE SHAPE AFTER THE "QUESTIONING" IS UNDER WAY,
IS ALMOST CERTAIN TO LEAD TO AIMLESSNESS AND
FAILURE.

H-19   B.   RESISTANCE BY THE SUBJECT

H-20   1.   WHAT TYPE AND INTENSITY OF RESISTANCE IS
        ANTICIPATED?

H-20   2.   IS THE INFORMATION DAMAGING TO THE SUBJECT
        IN ANY WAY?

H-20   3.   CAN THE INFORMATION BE OBTAINED FROM OTHER
        SOURCES?

H-20   4.   WHICH TECHNIQUES WILL PROBABLY BE MOST
        SUCCESSFUL IN OVERCOMING RESISTANCE?

H-20   5.   WHICH RATIONALIZATION WILL BEST AID THE
        SUBJECT IN OVERCOMING HIS RESISTANCE?

H-21   C.   THE "QUESTIONING" ROOM

H-22   1.   IS THE ROOM FREE OF DISTRACTIONS?

H-22   2.   ARE THE FURNISHINGS CONDUCIVE TO THE DESIRED
        MOOD?

H-22   3.   ARE THERE WARNING LIGHTS TO PREVENT
        INTERRUPTIONS?

H-22   4.   ARE THERE PROVISIONS FOR OUTSIDE VIEWING AND
        RECORDING?

H-22   5.   ARE THERE PROVISIONS FOR RESTRAINTS IF
        REQUIRED? .

H-22   6.   ARE THERE PROVISIONS FOR REFRESHMENTS IF
        REQUIRED?

H-23 D. THE PARTICIPANTS

H-24 1. WILL THE SUBJECT BE "QUESTIONED" ALONE OR
JOINTLY WITH OTHER SUBJECTS? SEPARATE
"QUESTIONING" INCREASES A SUBJECT'S FEELING OF
BEING CUT OFF FROM FRIENDLY AID AND PERMITS THE
USE OF A NUMBER OF TECHNIQUES THAT WOULD NOT BE
POSSIBLE OTHERWISE.

CONFRONTATION OF TWO SUBJECTS IN ORDER TO PRODUCE
ADMISSIONS IS ESPECIALLY DANGEROUS IF NOT
PRECEEDED BY SEPARATE "QUESTIONING" SESSIONS
WHICH HAVE EVOKED COMPLIANCE FROM ONE OF THE
SUBJECTS.

H-24 2. WILL THERE BE MORE THAN ONE "QUESTIONER"?
IF SO. HOW WILL THE TEAM FUNCTION? HAVE ROLES
BEEN ASSIGNED AND REHEARSED? THE "QUESTIONER"
MUST BE ABLE TO FUNCTION ON TWO LEVELS. HE MUST
ACHIEVE RAPPORT WITH THE SUBJECT BUT REMAIN A
DETACHED OBSERVER, WHOLLY UNCOMMITTED AT A DEEPER
LEVEL, NOTING THE SIGNIFICANCE OF THE SUBJECT'S
REACTIONS AND THE EFFECTIVENESS OF HIS OWN
PERFORMANCE.

H-24 WHAT OTHER SUPPORT WILL BE REQUIRED?
INTERPRETER. DOCTOR. PSYCHIATRIST. MATRON,
ANALYST. ETC.

H-24   4.   HAVE POSSIBLE REASONS FOR CHANGING

"QUESTIONERS" BEEN ANTICIPATED AND PLANNED FOR?

IF THE RELATIONSHIP BETWEEN THE FIRST

"QUESTIONER" AND THE SUBJECT IS DESTROYED BY A

CHANGE IN "QUESTIONERS", THE REPLACEMENT MUST NOT

ONLY START FROM SCRATCH BUT ACTUALLY STARTS WITH

A HANDICAP. BECAUSE THE SUBJECT'S PREVIOUS

EXPOSURE TO "QUESTIONING" WILL HAVE MADE HIM A

MORE EFFECTIVE RESISTER.

H-24   5.   HAS THE "QUESTIONER" DETERMINED HIS

BARGAINING POSITION?

H-24   6.   HAS THE "QUESTIONER" OBTAINED APPROVAL FOR

ANY COERCIVE TECHNIQUES TO BE USED?

H-25   E.   THE TIMING

H-26   1.   WHAT IS THE ESTIMATED TIME TO ACCOMPLISH THE

OBJECTIVES OF THE "QUESTIONING"?

H-26   2.   HOW MUCH TIME IS AVAILABLE TO THE

"QUESTIONER" FOR DETENTION OF THE SUBJECT?

H-26   HAS A COMPLETE SCHEDULE OF SESSIONS BEEN

PLANNED?   "QUESTIONING" OF A RESISTANT SUBJECT

SHOULD BE DONE ON A VARYING SCHEDULE SO AS TO

DISRUPT HIS SENSE OF CHRONOLOGICAL ORDER.

DISORIENTATION WILL REDUCE HIS CAPACITY FOR

RESISTANCE.

H-27 THE TERMINATION

H-28 1.   THE TERMINATION PHASE SHOULD BE CONSIDERED
BEFORE "QUESTIONING" EVER STARTS.   THE TECHNIQUES
USED AND EVEN THE OBJECTIVE OF THE "QUESTIONING"
MAY BE SHAPED BY THE PLANNED EMPLOYMENT OF THE
SUBJECT.

H-28 ~~2.   HAS PSYCHOLOGICAL REGRESSION BEEN INDUCED?~~

H-28 2.   WILL HE SIMPLY BE RELEASED?   IF SO, WILL HE
BE ABLE TO CAUSE EMBARRASSMENT BY GOING TO THE
NEWSPAPERS OR COURTS?   SPENDING THE EXTRA TIME
WITH HIM TO REPLACE HIS SENSE OF EMPTINESS WITH
NEW VALUES CAN BE GOOD INSURANCE.   WILL A
QUIT-CLAIM BE OBTAINED?

H-28 3. 4.   · WILL HE BE TURNED OVER TO ANOTHER SERVICE?
IF SO. HOLD TO A MINIMUM THE INFORMATION ABOUT
YOUR SERVICE AND YOUR METHODS THAT HE CAN
COMMUNICATE.

H-28 4. 5.   IS OPERATIONAL USE CONTEMPLATED?   HOW WILL
HE BE PHASED INTO THE OPERATION?   IF HE IS TO BE
RETURNED TO HIS ORGANIZATION TO WORK AGAINST HIS
EX-COLLEAGUES. HE MUST BE RETURNED QUICKLY SO AS
NOT TO BE MISSED.   HAVE RECONTACT ARRANGEMENTS
BEEN MADE?   HOW IS HE TO BE PAID?

CONDUCTING THE "QUESTIONING"
                    ===-=========-------==-=====

   I.   STRUCTURE OF THE "QUESTIONING"

        THERE ARE FOUR PHASES IN A "QUESTIONING".

I-1   A.   THE OPENING

              A PRINCIPAL GOAL DURING THE OPENING PHASE IS TO

              CONFIRM THE PERSONALITY ASSESSMENT MADE DURING

              SCREENING AND TO GAIN A DEEPER UNDERSTANDING OF

              THE SUBJECT. UNLESS TIME IS CRUCIAL, THE SUBJECT

              IS ALLOWED TO TALK WITHOUT INTERRUPTION. HE MAY

              REVEAL SIGNIFICANT FACTS WHICH WERE PREVIOUSLY

              OVERLOOKED.
                                                    ..

              A SECOND GOAL IS TO ESTABLISH RAPPORT. A LACK OF

              RAPPORT MAY CAUSE A SUBJECT TO WITHHOLD

              INFORMATION THAT HE WOULD HAVE PROVIDED FREELY.

              ESTABLISHING RAPPORT MAY INDUCE A SUBJECT WHO IS

              DETERMINED TO WITHHOLD INFORMATION TO CHANGE HIS

              ATTITUDE. THE "QUESTIONER" SHOULD NOT BE

              DISSUADED FROM THE EFFORT TO ESTABLISH RAPPORT BY

              THE BELIEF THAT NO MAN IN HIS RIGHT MIND WOULD

              INCRIMINATE HIMSELF. THE HISTORY OF

              "QUESTIONING" IS FULL OF CONFESSIONS AND

              SELF-INCRIMINATIONS.

THE "QUESTIONER" SHOULD REMAIN BUSINESS-LIKE BUT
ALSO FRIENDLY. HE SHOULD AVOID BEING DRAWN INTO
A CONFLICT OF PERSONALITIES WHERE THE SELF-ESTEEM
OF THE SUBJECT IS INVOLVED. HOSTILITY FROM THE
SUBJECT IS BEST HANDLED BY A CALM INTEREST IN
WHAT HAS AROUSED HIM, i.e. "WHY DON'T YOU TELL ME
WHAT HAS MADE YOU ANGRY?"

DURING THE OPENING PHASE THE "QUESTIONER" TRIES
TO DETERMINE THE CAUSE FOR ANY RESISTANCE BY THE
SUBJECT. USUALLY, IT IS FOR ONE OF FOUR REASONS:
1) A SPECIFIC NEGATIVE REACTION TO THE
"QUESTIONER".
2) RESISTANCE "BY NATURE" TO ANY COMPLIANCE WITH
AUTHORITY.
3) INFORMATION SOUGHT IS DAMAGING OR
INCRIMINATING.
4) IDEOLOGICAL RESISTANCE BECAUSE OF A BELIEF IN
A CAUSE.

THE "QUESTIONER" WHO SENSES DURING THE OPENING
PHASE THAT HE IS HEARING A COVER STORY SHOULD
RESIST THE NATURAL IMPULSE TO DEMONSTRATE ITS
FALSITY. IT IS BETTER TO LEAVE AN AVENUE OF
ESCAPE, A MEANS BY WHICH THE SUBJECT CAN CORRECT
HIS STORY WITHOUT LOOKING FOOLISH.

IF IT IS DECIDED TO CONFRONT THE SUBJECT WITH PROOF OF LYING LATER DURING THE "QUESTIONING", IT SHOULD BE DONE IN A MANNER SIMILAR TO CROSS EXAMINATION IN COURT. FOR INSTANCE, A WITNESS WOULD BE CONFRONTED WITH A LIE IN SUCH A WAY THAT HE COULD NEITHER DENY IT NOR EXPLAIN IT. IF YOU HAD A LETTER WRITTEN BY A WITNESS IN WHICH HE TAKES THE OPPOSITE POSITION ON SOMETHING HE HAS JUST SWORN TO. YOU WOULD NOT JUST READ IT TO HIM WITH THE INQUIRY, "WHAT DO YOU HAVE TO SAY TO THAT?" THE CORRECT METHOD WOULD BE TO LEAD THE WITNESS INTO REPEATING THE STATEMENTS WHICH HIS LETTER CONTRADICTS. THEN READ THE LETTER TO HIM WITHOUT ALLOWING HIM TO EXPLAIN.

HOW LONG THE OPENING PHASE CONTINUES DEPENDS UPON HOW LONG IT TAKES TO ESTABLISH RAPPORT OR TO DETERMINE THAT COOPERATION IS UNOBTAINABLE.

I-3   B.   THE RECONNAISSANCE

IF RAPPORT HAS BEEN ESTABLISHED AND THE SUBJECT

IS COOPERATIVE, THEN THIS PHASE CAN BE BYPASSED.

BUT IF HE IS WITHHOLDING, THE PURPOSE OF THE

RECONNAISSANCE IS TO PROBE THE CAUSES, EXTENT,

AND INTENSITY OF HIS RESISTANCE TO DETERMINE THE

KIND AND DEGREE OF PRESSURE THAT WILL BE NEEDED

DURING THE THIRD PHASE.

I-4   TWO DANGERS ARE LIKELY TO APPEAR DURING THE

RECONNAISSANCE. UNTIL NOW THE "QUESTIONER" HAS

NOT CONTINUED A LINE OF QUESTIONING WHEN

RESISTANCE WAS MET, BUT NOW, AS HE KEEPS COMING

BACK TO AREAS OF SENSITIVITY, RAPPORT MAY BE

STRAINED AND THE SUBJECT MAY ATTEMPT TO

PERSONALIZE THE CONFLICT. THE "QUESTIONER" MUST

RESIST THIS ATTEMPT.

THE SECOND DANGER IS THE NATURAL INCLINATION TO

RESORT TO RUSES TO GET THE "QUESTIONING" OVER

WITH IN A HURRY. THE PURPOSE OF THE

RECONNAISSANCE IS TO PROBE. THE "QUESTIONER"

SHOULD RESERVE HIS FIRE-POWER UNTIL HE KNOWS WHAT

HE IS UP AGAINST.

I-5   C.   THE DETAILED QUESTIONING

             MAJOR CONSIDERATIONS INCLUDE:

I-6   1)   KNOW WHAT THE SPECIFIC REQUIREMENTS ARE AND
             WHAT QUESTIONS YOU WANT TO USE.

I-7   KEEP THE QUESTIONING FOCUSED ON THE
             REQUIREMENTS.

I-8   3)   COVER ALL ELEMENTS OF WHO, WHAT, WHEN,
             WHERE, WHY, HOW.

I-9   4)   DETERMINE IF THE SUBJECT'S KNOWLEDGE IS
             FIRST HAND, LEARNED INDIRECTLY, OR MERELY
             ASSUMPTION. IF LEARNED INDIRECTLY, OBTAIN
             IDENTITIES OF SUB-SOURCES. IF ASSUMPTION, GET
             THE FACTS UPON WHICH IT IS BASED.

I-10   5)   CONTINUE TO REEXAMINE THE SUBJECT'S
             BIOGRAPHIC HISTORY, OVER AND OVER, IN MORE AND
             MORE DETAIL.

I-11   6)   COVER GAPS OR DISCREPANCIES NOTED IN
             PREVIOUS SESSIONS.

I-12   7)   MAKE NOTES OF TOPICS TO BE EXPLORED LATER.
             THEY TEND TO DISRUPT THE PLAN IF COVERED AS THEY
             POP UP.

I-13   8)   EXPECT THE SUBJECT'S PSYCHOLOGICAL CONDITION
             TO VARY PERIODICALLY AND VARY YOUR TECHNIQUE

I-14   9)   FROM THE BEGINNING TO THE END OF THE

"QUESTIONING" MAKE THE SUBJECT FEEL THAT YOUR

INTEREST IN HIM HAS REMAINED CONSTANT.

I-15   THINGS TO AVOID DURING THE DETAILED QUESTIONING:

I-15   1)   DO NOT ALLOW THE SUBJECT TO DETERMINE YOUR

EXACT AREA OF INTEREST.

I-16   2)   DO NOT ALLOW THE SUBJECT TO DETERMINE THE

EXTENT OF YOUR KNOWLEDGE.

I-17   3)   DO NOT GIVE THE SUBJECT A LIST OF QUESTIONS

AND ASK HIM TO ANSWER THEM.

I-18   4)   DO NOT ASK QUESTIONS REQUIRING "YES" OR "NO"

ANSWERS.

I-19   5)   DO NOT PUSH THE "QUESTIONING" BEYOND THE

RATE PLANNED. REMEMBER. TIME IS ON YOUR SIDE.

I-20   OTHER CONSIDERATIONS

I-20   IDEOLOGICAL ARGUMENT

THE "QUESTIONER" SHOULD BE PREPARED TO DISCUSS

THE PRINCIPLES OF AND OFFER VALID ALTERNATIVES TO

THE IDEOLOGY THAT MOTIVATED THE SUBJECT TO SELECT

HIS PARTICULAR COURSE OF ACTION. THE PURPOSE OF

THIS DISCUSSION IS NOT TO PROVE THE SUBJECT WRONG

BUT TO PROVIDE HIM WITH REASONS WHICH HE CAN USE

TO JUSTIFY TO HIMSELF FOR CHANGING SIDES.

BARGAINING.

HAVING THE PROPER APPROVAL TO BARGAIN WITH THE SUBJECT. TO BE ABLE TO OFFER HIM SOMETHING IN EXCHANGE FOR HIS COOPERATION CAN SAVE WEEKS OF EFFORT. PRIOR TO CONDUCTING THE "QUESTIONING", THE "QUESTIONER" MUST BE VERY SURE AS TO WHAT OFFERS MAY BE MADE AND WHAT MAY NOT.

EXAMPLES OF WHAT THE SUBJECT MAY ASK:

1)   WHAT CAN YOU DO FOR HIM IF HE COOPERATES?

2)   WHAT WILL HAPPEN TO HIM IF HE DOES NOT?

3)   CAN YOU PROTECT HIM FROM RETALIATION?

EXAMPLES OF OFFERS THE "QUESTIONER" CAN MAKE:

1)   PROTECTION

2)   NEW IDENTITY

3)   RELOCATION TO ANOTHER COUNTRY

4)   CHANCE TO WORK AGAINST FORMER COLLEAGUES

A THREAT IS BASICALLY A MEANS FOR ESTABLISHING A

BARGAINING POSTION BY INDUCING FEAR IN THE

SUBJECT. A THREAT SHOULD NEVER BE MADE UNLESS IT

IS PART OF THE PLAN AND THE "QUESTIONER" HAS THE

APPROVAL TO CARRY OUT THE THREAT. WHEN A THREAT

IS USED. IT SHOULD ALWAYS BE IMPLIED THAT THE

SUBJECT HIMSELF IS TO BLAME BY USING WORDS SUCH

AS, "YOU LEAVE ME NO OTHER CHOICE BUT TO ...."

HE SHOULD NEVER BE TOLD TO COMPLY "OR ELSE!"

EXAMPLES OF THREATS:

1)   TURN HIM OVER TO LOCAL AUTHORITIES FOR LEGAL

ACTION

2)   RETURN HIM TO HIS ORGANIZATION AFTER

COMPROMISING HIM

3)   PUBLIC EXPOSURE

4)   DEPRIVATIONS OF PRISON
      AS CIGARETTES

5)   DEPORTATION

6)   CONFISCATION OF PROPERTY

7)   PHYSICAL VIOLENCE   ✓

I-23   D.   THE TERMINATION

        THE DISPOSITION OF THE SUBJECT MUST BE PLANNED

        BEFORE THE "QUESTIONING" EVER STARTS. BE SURE TO

        CONSIDER ALL THE POINTS COVERED UNDER "THE

        TERMINATION" DURING THE LESSON ON PLANNING.

        YOU MUST GUARD AGAINST ANY POSSIBLE TROUBLE
                                        THE BEST DEFENSE
        CAUSED BY A VENGEFUL SUBJECT.

        IS PREVENTION, THROUGH ENLISTMENT OR COMPROMISE.

        THE DETAILED QUESTIONING ENDS ONLY WHEN:

I-24   1).   YOU HAVE OBTAINED ALL USEFUL INFORMATION.

I-25   2)   YOU HAVE MORE PRESSING REQUIREMENTS.

I-26   3)   YOU ARE READY TO ADMIT DEFEAT.

   III. CONCLUSION

        REMEMBER, THE "QUESTIONER" ALWAYS HAS THE ADVANTAGE IN

   A "QUESTIONING". HE KNOWS MORE ABOUT THE SUBJECT THAN

   THE SUBJECT KNOWS ABOUT HIM. HE CREATES, MODIFIES,

   AMPLIFIES, AND TERMINATES THE SUBJECT'S ENVIRONMENT.

   HE SELECTS THE EMOTIONAL KEYS UNDER WHICH THE

   "QUESTIONING" WILL PROCEED. THE SUBJECT IS ACUTELY

   AWARE THAT THE "QUESTIONER" CONTROLS HIS ULTIMATE

   DISPOSITION.

NON-COERCIVE TECHNIQUES

I. GENERAL

A.   SUBJECTS MAKE ADMISSIONS OR CONFESSONS BECAUSE
THEY ARE IN A STATE OF MIND WHICH LEADS THEM TO
BELIEVE THAT COOPERATION IS THE BEST COURSE OF ACTION
FOR THEM TO FOLLOW. THE EFFECTIVE USE OF THE PROPER
"QUESTIONING" TECHNIQUE WILL AID IN DEVELOPING THIS
STATE OF MIND.

K-1   B.   ALL NON-COERCIVE "QUESTIONING" TECHNIQUES ARE
BASED ON THE PRINCIPLE OF GENERATING PRESSURE INSIDE
THE SUBJECT WITHOUT THE APPLICATION OF OUTSIDE FORCE.
THIS IS ACCOMPLISHED BY MANIPULATING HIM
PSYCHOLOGICALLY UNTIL HIS RESISTANCE IS SAPPED AND HIS
URGE TO YIELD IS FORTIFIED.

C.   THE EFFECTIVENESS OF MOST "QUESTIONING"
TECHNIQUES DEPENDS UPON THEIR UNSETTLING EFFECT. THE
"QUESTIONING" PROCESS ITSELF IS UNSETTLING TO MOST
PEOPLE ENCOUNTERING IT FOR THE FIRST TIME. THE
"QUESTIONER" TRIES TO ENHANCE THIS EFFECT, TO DISRUPT
RADICALLY THE FAMILIAR EMOTIONAL AND PSYCHOLOGICAL
ASSOCIATIONS OF THE SUBJECT.

D. ONCE THIS DISRUPTION IS ACHIEVED. THE SUBJECT'S
RESISTANCE IS SERIOUSLY IMPAIRED. HE EXPERIENCES A
KIND OF PSYCHOLOGICAL SHOCK, WHICH MAY ONLY LAST
BRIEFLY, BUT DURING WHICH HE IS FAR MORE OPEN TO
SUGGESTION AND FAR LIKELIER TO COMPLY, THAN HE WAS
BEFORE HE EXPERIENCED THE SHOCK.

E. FREQUENTLY THE SUBJECT WILL EXPERIENCE A FEELING
OF GUILT. IF THE "QUESTIONER" CAN INTENSIFY THESE
GUILT FEELINGS, IT WILL INCREASE THE SUBJECT'S
ANXIETY AND HIS URGE TO COOPERATE AS A MEANS OF ESCAPE.

F. THE INITIAL ADVANTAGE ALWAYS LIES WITH THE
"QUESTIONER". FROM THE OUTSET, HE KNOWS A GREAT DEAL
MORE ABOUT THE SUBJECT THAN THE SUBJECT KNOWS ABOUT
HIM. HE IS ABLE TO MANIPULATE THE SUBJECT'S
ENVIRONMENT, TO CREATE UNPLEASANT OR INTOLERABLE
SITUATIONS, TO DISRUPT PATTERNS OF TIME, SPACE, AND
SENSORY PERCEPTION. THE SUBJECT IS VERY MUCH AWARE
THAT THE "QUESTIONER" CONTROLS HIS ULTIMATE DISPOSITON.

G. THE NUMBER OF VARIATIONS IN TECHNIQUES IS LIMITED
ONLY BY THE EXPERIENCE AND IMAGINATION OF THE
"QUESTIONER". THE SUCCESS AND SKILL OF AN EXPERIENCED
"QUESTIONER" LIE IN HIS ABILITY TO MATCH THE TECHNIQUE
SELECTED TO THE PERSONALITY OF THE SUBJECT AND HIS
RAPID EXPLOITATION AT THE MOMENT OF SHOCK.

H.   THE "QUESTIONER" SHOULD NOT TRY VARIOUS TECHNIQUES UNTIL HE FINDS ONE THAT WORKS.   THE USE OF UNSUCCESSFUL TECHNIQUES WILL IN ITSELF INCREASE THE SUBJECT'S WILL AND ABILITY TO RESIST.

I.   IF IN THE OPINION OF THE "QUESTIONER", A SUBJECT HAS THE WILL AND DETERMINATION TO WITHSTAND ALL NON-COERCIVE TECHNIQUES, IT IS BETTER TO AVOID THEM COMPLETELY.

II. TECHNIQUES

A.   THE DIRECT APPROACH

THE "QUESTIONER" MAKES NO EFFORT TO CONCEAL THE PURPOSE OF THE "QUESTIONING" BECAUSE HE FEELS THE SUBJECT WILL OFFER LITTLE OR NO RESISTANCE.   ITS ADVANTAGE IS THAT IT IS SIMPLE AND TAKES LITTLE TIME.   IT HAS PROVEN EFFECTIVE WITH LOW LEVEL SOURCES WITH LITTLE OR NO SECURITY TRAINING.   IT IS ALSO USED WITH A SUBJECT WHO HAS PROVEN COOPERATIVE DURING A PREVIOUS SESSION.

B.   GOING NEXT DOOR

OCCASIONALLY THE INFORMATION NEEDED FROM A RESISTANT SUBJECT IS OBTAINABLE FROM ANOTHER, MORE WILLING SOURCE.   THE "QUESTIONER" MUST DECIDE WHETHER THE INFORMATION ITSELF IS HIS GOAL OR WHETHER A CONFESSION IS ESSENTIAL FOR OPERATIONAL CONSIDERATIONS.

K-4   C.   NOBODY LOVES YOU

A SUBJECT WHO IS WITHHOLDING INFORMATION OF NO
GRAVE CONSEQUENCE TO HIMSELF MAY SOMETIMES BE
PERSUADED TO TALK BY POINTING OUT THAT EVERYTHING
CONCERNING HIS CASE HAS BEEN LEARNED FROM PERSONS
WHO MAY BE BIASED OR MALICIOUS.   THE SUBJECT OWES
IT TO HIMSELF TO BE SURE THE "QUESTIONER" HEARS
BOTH SIDES OF THE STORY, OR ELSE HE MAY BE
SENTENCED ON THE TESTIMONY OF PERSONAL ENEMIES
WITHOUT A WORD IN HIS OWN DEFENSE.

K-5   D.   WE KNOW EVERYTHING

THE "QUESTIONER" EXPLAINS TO THE SUBJECT THAT HE
ALREADY KNOWS EVERYTHING, THAT THE PURPOSE OF THE
"QUESTIONING" IS NOT TO GAIN INFORMATION, BUT TO
TEST THE SINCERITY (HONOR, RELIABILITY, ETC.) OF
THE SUBJECT.   THE "QUESTIONER" THEN ASKS
QUESTIONS BASED ON KNOWN DATA.   IF THE SUBJECT
LIES, HE IS INFORMED FIRMLY AND DISPASSIONATELY
THAT HE HAS LIED.

A FILE OR DOSSIER CAN BE PREPARED CONTAINING ALL AVAILABLE INFORMATION CONCERNING THE SUBJECT OR HIS ORGANIZATION. IT CAN BE PADDED WITH EXTRA PAPER, IF NECESSARY, TO GIVE THE ILLUSION THAT IT CONTAINS MORE DATA THAN IS ACTUALLY THERE. IT SHOULD HAVE INDEX TABS SUCH AS: "EDUCATION, "EMPLOYMENT", "CRIMINAL RECORD". "MILITARY SERVICE", ETC.

THE "QUESTIONER" CONFRONTS THE SUBJECT WITH THE DOSSIER AND EXPLAINS.THAT HE HAS A COMPLETE RECORD OF EVERY SIGNIFICANT HAPPENING IN THE SUBJECT'S LIFE. HE MAY EVEN READ A FEW SELECTED BITS OF INFORMATION TO FURTHER IMPRESS THE SUBJECT.

BY MANIPULATING THE KNOWN FACTS. THE "QUESTIONER" MAY BE ABLE TO CONVINCE A NAIVE SUBJECT THAT ALL HIS SECRETS ARE OUT AND THAT FURTHER RESISTANCE IS POINTLESS. HOWEVER, IF THIS TECHNIQUE DOES NOT WORK QUICKLY, IT MUST BE DROPPED BEFORE THE SUBJECT LEARNS THE TRUE LIMITS OF THE "QUESTIONER'S" KNOWLEDGE.

E   DOUBLE INFORMERS

PLANTING AN INFORMANT IN A SUBJECT'S CELL IS A
WELL-KNOWN TRICK. .LESS WELL KNOWN IS THE TRICK
OF PLANTING TWO INFORMANTS (A & B) IN THE SAME
CELL. NOW AND THEN. "A" TRIES TO PRY A LITTLE
INFORMATION FROM THE SUBJECT. AT THE PROPER
TIME, AND DURING A'S ABSENCE, "B" WARNS THE
SUBJECT NOT TO TELL "A" ANYTHING BECAUSE "B"
SUSPECTS HIM OF BEING AN INFORMANT.

(SUSPICION AGAINST A SINGLE INFORMANT MAY
SOMETIMES BE DISPELLED IF HE SHOWS THE SUBJECT A
HIDDEN MICROPHONE THAT HE HAS "FOUND" AND
SUGGESTS THAT THEY TALK ONLY IN WHISPERS AT THE
OTHER END OF THE ROOM)

K-7   *F*   NEWS FROM HOME

ALLOWING A SUBJECT TO RECEIVE CAREFULLY SELECTED
LETTERS FROM HOME CAN HELP CREATE AN EFFECT
DESIRED BY THE "QUESTIONER". FOR EXAMPLE, THE
SUBJECT MAY GET THE IDEA THAT HIS RELATIVES ARE
UNDER DURESS OR SUFFERING. A SUGGESTION AT THE
PROPER TIME, THAT HIS COOPERATION OR CONFESSION
CAN HELP PROTECT THE INNOCENT MAY BE EFFECTIVE.

IF THE SUBJECT CAN BE LED TO BELIEVE THAT LETTERS
CAN BE SMUGGLED OUT WITHOUT THE KNOWLEDGE OF THE
AUTHORITIES. THE LETTERS HE WRITES MAY PRODUCE
INFORMATION WHICH IS DIFFICULT TO EXTRACT BY
DIRECT QUESTIONING.

K-8   G.   THE WITNESS

1.   A WITNESS CAN BE ESCORTED INTO AN INNER
OFFICE PAST THE SUBJECT IN AN OUTER OFFICE
WITHOUT ALLOWING THEM TO SPEAK TO EACH OTHER.
AFTER AN HOUR, A STENOGRAPHER IS CALLED IN FROM
THE OUTER OFFICE, TO GIVE THE IMPRESSION SHE IS
TAKING A STATEMENT. SHE LATER RE-EMERGES AND
TYPES THE STATEMENT IN THE OUTER OFFICE.. SHE
TELEPHONES FOR SOMEONE TO COME IN TO ACT AS LEGAL
WITNESS, AND TAKES THE COMPLETED WORK INTO THE
INNER OFFICE. THEN THE "QUESTIONER" EMERGES AND
INSTRUCTS THE GUARD TO TAKE THE SUBJECT BACK TO
HIS CELL STATING, "WE DON'T NEED HIM ANY MORE."
EVEN IF THE SUBJECT INSISTS ON TELLING HIS SIDE
OF THE STORY, HE IS TOLD TO RELAX BECAUSE THE
"QUESTIONER" WILL GET AROUND TO HIM TOMORROW OR
THE NEXT DAY.

2. A COOPERATIVE WITNESS CAN SOMETIMES BE COACHED TO EXAGGERATE THE SUBJECT'S INVOLVEMENT OR ACCUSE HIM OF A WORSE CRIME THAN THE MATTER AT HAND. UPON HEARING THESE REMARKS FROM A RECORDING, A SUBJECT MAY CONFESS THE TRUTH ABOUT THE LESSER GUILT IN ORDER TO PROVIDE HIMSELF WITH AN ALIBI.

3.   IF THE WITNESS REFUSES TO DENOUNCE THE SUBJECT, THE "QUESTIONER" ELICITS AND RECORDS REMARKS FROM HIM DENOUNCING SOMEONE ELSE KNOWN TO HIM, FOR EXAMPLE, A CRIMINAL WHO WAS RECENTLY CONVICTED IN COURT. DURING THE NEXT SESSION WITH THE SUBJECT, THESE REMARKS, EDITED AS NECESSARY, ARE PLAYED BACK SO THAT THE SUBJECT IS PERSUADED THAT HE IS THE SUBJECT OF THE REMARKS.

H.   JOINT SUSPECTS (AKA DIVIDE AND CONQUER)

IF TWO OR MORE SUBJECTS ARE SUSPECTED OF JOINT

COMPLICITY, THEY SHOULD BE SEPARATED IMMEDIATELY.

IF TIME PERMITS, "QUESTIONING" SHOULD BE

POSTPONED FOR ABOUT A WEEK. ANY ANXIOUS

INQUIRIES FROM ONE SUBJECT SHOULD BE MET WITH A

REPLY SUCH AS, "WE'LL GET TO YOU IN DUE TIME.

THERE'S NO HURRY NOW!". IF DOCUMENTS, WITNESSES,

OR OTHER SOURCES YIELD INFORMATION ABOUT SUBJECT

"B", SUCH INFORMATION SHOULD BE ATTRIBUTED TO

SUBJECT "A" TO GIVE "B" THE IMPRESSION THAT "A"

IS TALKING.

IF THE "QUESTIONER" IS QUITE CERTAIN OF THE FACTS

BUT CANNOT SECURE AN ADMISSION FROM EITHER

SUBJECT, A WRITTEN CONFESSION MAY BE PREPARED

WITH A'S SIGNATURE REPRODUCED ON IT. THE

CONFESSION CONTAINS ALL THE SALIENT FACTS BUT

THEY ARE DISTORTED. IT SHOWS THAT "A" IS

ATTEMPTING TO THROW THE ENTIRE BLAME ON "B".

(EDITED TAPE RECORDINGS WHICH SOUND AS IF "A" IS

DENOUNCING "B" CAN ALSO ACCOMPLISH THE SAME

PURPOSE)

THE INNER-AND-OUTER OFFICE ROUTINE MAY ALSO BE

EMPLOYED WITH "A", THE WEAKER, BEING BROUGHT INTO

THE INNER OFFICE, AND GIVING "B" IN THE OUTER

OFFICE THE IMPRESSION HE IS TALKING.

WHEN THE "QUESTIONER" IS FAIRLY CERTAIN THAT "B"
IS CONVINCED THAT "A" HAS BROKEN DOWN AND TOLD
HIS STORY HE TELLS "B", "SINCE "A" HAS COOPERATED
WITH US, HE WILL BE RELEASED, BUT IT SEEMS THAT
HE WAS PRETTY ANGRY WITH YOU AND FEELS THAT YOU
GOT HIM INTO THIS JAM. HE MIGHT EVEN GO BACK TO
YOUR SUPERIORS AND SAY THAT YOU HAVEN'T RETURNED
BECAUSE YOU HAVE DECIDED TO STAY HERE AND WORK
FOR US. WOULDN'T IT BE BETTER FOR YOU IF I SET
YOU BOTH FREE TOGETHER? WOULDN'T IT BE BETTER TO
TELL ME YOUR SIDE OF THE STORY?"

IT IS IMPORTANT THAT IN ALL SUCH GAMBITS, "A" BE
THE WEAKER OF THE TWO, EMOTIONALLY AND
PSYCHOLOGICALLY.

K-10   I.   JOINT "QUESTIONERS" (AKA FRIEND AND FOE)

THE COMMONEST OF THE JOINT "QUESTIONERS"
TECHNIQUES IS THE "FRIEND AND FOE" ROUTINE. THE
TWO "QUESTIONERS" DISPLAY OPPOSING PERSONALITIES
AND ATTITUDES TOWARD THE SUBJECT. FOR EXAMPLE
THE FIRST "QUESTIONER" DISPLAYS AN UNSYMPATHETIC
ATTITUDE TOWARD THE SUBJECT. HE MAY BE BRUTAL,
ANGRY, OR DOMINEERING. HE MAKES IT PLAIN THAT HE
CONSIDERS THE SUBJECT THE VILEST PERSON ON EARTH.
HIS GOAL IS TO ALIENATE THE SUBJECT. AT THE
HEIGHT OF THE ALIENATION, THE SECOND "QUESTIONER"
TAKES OVER, SENDING THE FIRST OUT OF THE ROOM.

THE SECOND "QUESTIONER" THEN DISPLAYS A SYMPATHETIC ATTITUDE TOWARD THE SUBJECT, PERHAPS OFFERING HIM COFFEE AND A CIGARETTE. HE EXPLAINS THAT THE ACTIONS OF THE FIRST "QUESTIONER" WERE LARGELY THE RESULT OF HIS LACK OF KNOWLEDGE IN DEALING WITH PEOPLE AND LACK OF HUMAN SENSITIVITY. IF BRUTES LIKE THAT WOULD KEEP QUIET AND GIVE A MAN A FAIR CHANCE TO TELL HIS SIDE OF THE STORY, ETC., ETC.

THE SUBJECT IS NORMALLY INCLINED TO HAVE A FEELING OF GRATITUDE TOWARDS THE SECOND "QUESTIONER", WHO CONTINUES TO DISPLAY A SYMPATHETIC ATTITUDE IN AN EFFORT TO ENHANCE THE RAPPORT FOR THE "QUESTIONING" WHICH WILL FOLLOW. IF THE SUBJECT'S COOPERATIVENESS BEGINS TO FADE, THE SECOND "QUESTIONER" CAN STATE THAT HE CANNOT AFFORD TO WASTE TIME ON SOURCES WHO FAIL TO COOPERATE AND IMPLY THAT THE FIRST "QUESTIONER" MIGHT RETURN TO CONTINUE THE "QUESTIONING".

WHEN THIS TECHNIQUE IS EMPLOYED AGAINST THE PROPER SOURCE. IT WILL NORMALLY GAIN THE SOURCE'S COMPLETE COOPERATION. IT WORKS BEST WITH WOMEN, TEENAGERS. AND TIMID MEN.

K-11   J.   IVAN IS A DOPE

IT MAY BE USEFUL TO POINT OUT TO A SUBJECT THAT
HIS COVER STORY WAS ILL CONTRIVED, THAT HIS
ORGANIZATION BOTCHED THE JOB, THAT IT IS TYPICAL
OF HIS ORGANIZATION TO IGNORE THE WELFARE OF ITS
MEMBERS. THE "QUESTIONER" EXPLAINS THAT HE HAS
BEEN IMPRESSED BY THE SUBJECT'S COURAGE AND
INTELLIGENCE AND BLAMES THE SUBJECT'S SUPERIORS
FOR THE FIX HE IS IN. HE SELLS THE SUBJECT ON
THE IDEA THAT HE IS A TRUE FRIEND, WHO
UNDERSTANDS THE SUBJECT AND WILL LOOK AFTER HIS
WELFARE.

K-12   K.   UNANSWERABLE QUESTIONING

A SUBJECT IS SYSTEMATICALLY AND PERSISTENTLY
QUESTIONED ABOUT MATTERS OF HIGH POLICY, PERSONS
OF PROMINENCE, TECHNICAL DETAIL, ETC., FOR WHICH
HE DOES NOT KNOW THE ANSWER. FOR EXAMPLE, HE MAY
BE ASKED ABOUT KGB POLICY, THE RELATION OF THE
SERVICE TO ITS GOVERNMENT, ITS LIAISON
ARRANGEMENTS, ETC. WHEN HE COMPLAINS THAT HE
KNOWS NOTHING OF SUCH MATTERS, THE "QUESTIONER"
·INSISTS THAT HE WOULD HAVE TO KNOW, THAT EVEN THE
MOST STUPID MEN IN HIS POSITION KNOW. EVENTUALLY
THE SUBJECT IS ASKED A QUESTION TO WHICH HE DOES
KNOW THE ANSWER, AND HE FEELS TREMENDOUS RELIEF
AT BEING ABLE TO ANSWER THE QUESTION.

CHECKLIST FOR THE "QUESTIONING"

I. OBJECTIVES OF THE "QUESTIONING"

    A. WHAT IS THE PURPOSE OF THE "QUESTIONING"?

    B. IS THIS A VALID REASON FOR "QUESTIONING"?

    C. IS THIS "QUESTIONING" NECESSARY OR CAN THE
    INFORMATION BE OBTAINED FROM OTHER SOURCES?

II. LIMITATIONS ON CONDUCTING THE "QUESTIONING"

    A. IS THE SUBJECT TO BE ARRESTED? BY WHOM? IS THE
    ARREST LEGAL? IF DIFFICULTIES DEVELOP, WILL THE
    ARRESTING LIAISON SERVICE REVEAL YOUR INTEREST OR ROLE?

    B. IF THE SUBJECT IS TO BE DETAINED, HOW LONG MAY HE
    LEGALLY BE DETAINED?

    C. HAVE ALL LOCAL LAWS AFFECTING THE CONDUCT OF A
    JOINT OR UNILATERAL EXPLOITATION BEEN COMPILED AND
    CONSIDERED?

III. ASSESSMENT OF THE SUBJECT

A. HAS ALL AVAILABLE AND PERTINENT INFORMATION ABOUT THE SUBJECT BEEN ASSEMBLED AND STUDIED?

B. HAVE ALL APPROPRIATE DOCUMENTS CARRIED BY THE SUBJECT BEEN SUBJECTED TO TECHNICAL ANALYSIS?

C. HAVE BACKGROUND CHECKS AND TRACES BEEN RUN ON THE SUBJECT AND PERSONS CLOSELY ASSOCIATED WITH HIM BY EMOTIONAL, FAMILY OR BUSINESS TIES?

D. HAVE THE SUBJECT'S BONA FIDES BEEN VERIFIED?

E. HAS THE SUBJECT BEEN SCREENED? WHAT ARE HIS MAJOR PSYCHOLOGICAL CHARACTERISTICS? IN WHICH OF THE NINE MAJOR CATEGORIES DOES HE BELONG?

F. IS IT ANTICIPATED THAT THE SUBJECT WILL BE COOPERATIVE OR RESISTANT? IF RESISTANCE IS EXPECTED, WHAT IS ITS PROBABLE SOURCE: FEAR, PATRIOTISM, POLITICAL CONVICTIONS, RELIGIOUS CONVICTIONS, STUBBORNESS, PERSONAL CONSIDERATIONS?

G. HAS THE SUBJECT BEEN "QUESTIONED" PREVIOUSLY? IS HE KNOWLEDGEABLE ABOUT SOPHISTICATED HOSTILE "QUESTIONING" TECHNIQUES?

IV. PLANNING THE "QUESTIONING"

A.   HAS A PLAN BEEN PREPARED?

B.   IF THE SUBJECT IS TO BE SENT TO A SPECIAL
FACILITY. HAS THE APPROVAL OF THE FACILITY CHIEF BEEN
OBTAINED?

C.   IF THE SUBJECT IS TO BE DETAINED ELSEWHERE, i.e.
A SAFEHOUSE. HAVE ARRANGEMENTS BEEN MADE TO FEED. BED,
AND GUARD HIM AS NECESSARY?

D.   IS AN APPROPRIATE SETTING FOR THE "QUESTIONING"
AVAILABLE?

E.   IS THE ENVIRONMENT WHERE THE SUBJECT IS TO BE
DETAINED AND "QUESTIONED" FULLY UNDER YOUR MANIPULATON
AND CONTROL?

F.   WILL THE DETENTION AND "QUESTIONING" FACILITIES
BE AVAILABLE FOR THE ENTIRE TIME ESTIMATED AS
NECESSARY TO COMPLETE THE EXPLOITATION?

G.   WILL THE SESSIONS BE RECORDED OR VIDEO TAPED?   IS
THE EQUIPMENT AVAILABLE AND INSTALLED?

H.   IF THE "QUESTIONING" IS TO BE CONDUCTED JOINTLY
WITH A LIAISON SERVICE, HAS DUE CONSIDERATION BEEN
GIVEN TO THE OPPORTUNITY THUS AFFORDED TO ACQUIRE
ADDITIONAL INFORMATION ABOUT THAT SERVICE WHILE
MINIMIZING EXPOSURE OF YOUR OWN SERVICE?

I. DOES THE "QUESTIONER" MEET THE FOLLOWING CRITERIA:

    1. ADEQUATE TRAINING AND EXPERIENCE?

    2. FAMILIARITY WITH THE LANGUAGE TO BE USED?

    3. KNOWLEDGE OF GEOGRAPHICAL AND CULTURAL AREAS?

    4. PSYCHOLOGICAL UNDERSTANDING OF THE SUBJECT?

J. IF MORE THAN ONE "QUESTIONER" IS CALLED FOR IN THE PLAN, HAVE ROLES BEEN ASSIGNED AND SCHEDULES PREPARED?

K. WHICH TECHNIQUES HAVE BEEN SELECTED FOR USE WITH THE SUBJECT?

    1. HOW WELL DO THEY MATCH THE SUBJECT'S PERSONALITY?

    2. IS SOLITARY CONFINEMENT TO BE USED? DOES THE PLACE OF CONFINEMENT PERMIT THE ELIMINATION OF SENSORY STIMULI?

    3. ARE THREATS TO BE USED? AS PART OF A PLAN? DOES THE NATURE OF THE THREAT MATCH THE PERSONALITY OF THE SUBJECT?

    4. ARE COERCIVE TECHNIQUES TO BE USED? HAVE ALL SUPERVISORS IN YOUR DIRECT CHAIN OF COMMAND BEEN NOTIFIED AND GIVEN APPROVAL? HAS HEADQUARTERS GIVEN APPROVAL?

V. CONDUCTING THE "QUESTIONING"

A. DURING THE OPENING PHASE, IS THERE AN EMOTIONAL REACTION ON EITHER YOUR PART OR THAT OF THE SUBJECT WHICH IS STRONG ENOUGH TO DISTORT THE RESULTS? IF SO, CAN YOU BE REPLACED WITH ANOTHER "QUESTIONER"?

B. DOES YOUR IMPRESSION OF THE SUBJECT CONFIRM OR CONFLICT WITH THE PRELIMINARY ASSESSMENT? IF THERE ARE SIGNIFICANT DIFFERENCES, HOW DO THEY AFFECT THE PLAN FOR THE REMAINDER OF THE "QUESTIONING"?

C. HAS RAPPORT BEEN ESTABLISHED?

D. HAVE THE SUBJECT'S EYES, MOUTH, VOICE, GESTURES, SILENCES, ETC. SUGGESTED AREAS OF SENSITIVITY? IF SO, ON WHAT TOPICS?

E. HAS THE OPENING PHASE BEEN FOLLOWED BY A RECONNAISANCE?

    1. WHAT ARE THE KEY AREAS OF RESISTANCE?

    2. WHAT TECHNIQUES AND HOW MUCH PRESSURE WILL BE REQUIRED TO OVERCOME THE RESISTANCE?

    3. SHOULD THE ESTIMATED DURATION OF THE "QUESTIONING" BE REVISED?

    4. ARE FURTHER ARRANGEMENTS NECESSARY FOR CONTINUED DETENTION, LIAISON SUPPORT OR OTHER PURPOSES?

F.   IF THE SUBJECT IS SUSPECTED OF MALINGERING. ARE THE SERVICES OF AN EXPERT AVAILABLE?

G.   IF THE SUBJECT HAS ADMITTED PRIOR ASSOCIATION WITH A FOREIGN INTELLIGENCE SERVICE. HAVE FULL DETAILS BEEN OBTAINED AND REPORTED?

H.   ARE REPORTS BEING MADE AFTER EACH SESSION?

VI.   TERMINATING THE "QUESTIONING"

A.   HAVE THE OBJECTIVES OF THE "QUESTIONING" BEEN MET?

B.   .HAS A COMPREHENSIVE SUMMARY REPORT BEEN PREPARED?

C.   HAVE ADMISSIONS BY THE SUBJECT BEEN RESEARCHED AND VERIFIED?

D.   IF DECEPTION IS DETECTED — RESUME THE "QUESTIONING"!

VII. EXPLOITATION AND DISPOSAL

A..   WHAT DISPOSITION OF THE SUBJECT IS TO BE MADE AFTER "QUESTIONING" ENDS?

1.   IF THE SUBJECT IS SUSPECTED OF BEING A HOSTILE AGENT, AND HE HAS NOT CONFESSED, WHAT MEASURES WILL BE TAKEN TO ENSURE THAT HE IS NOT ALLOWED TO OPERATE AS BEFORE?

2.   IF THE SUBJECT IS TO BE USED OPERATIONALLY, WHAT EFFECT (IF ANY) WILL THE "QUESTIONING" HAVE UPON THE OPERATION?

3.   IF THE SUBJECT IS TO BE TURNED OVER TO ANOTHER SERVICE, HOW MUCH WILL HE BE ABLE TO TELL THEM ABOUT YOUR SERVICE AND METHODS?

4.   IF THE SUBJECT IS TO BE TURNED OVER TO THE COURTS FOR PROSECUTION, WILL HE BE ABLE TO CAUSE EMBARRASSMENT TO YOUR SERVICE BECAUSE OF HIS DETENTION AND "QUESTIONING"?

B.   HAVE ANY PROMISES BEEN MADE TO THE SUBJECT WHICH ARE UNFULFILLED WHEN "QUESTIONING" ENDS? IS HE VENGEFUL OR LIKELY TO STRIKE BACK? HOW?

C.   HAS A QUIT-CLAIM BEEN OBTAINED?

D.   IF PSYCHOLOGICAL REGRESSION WAS INDUCED IN THE SUBJECT DURING THE "QUESTIONING" PROCESS, HOW IS IT PLANNED TO RESTORE HIM TO HIS ORIGINAL MENTAL CONDITION?

E.   WAS THE "QUESTIONING" SUCCESSFUL? WHY?

F.   A FAILURE? WHY?

REPORTING

I. GENERAL

REMEMBER THAT THE "QUESTIONING" IS NOT AN END IN
ITSELF; IT IS ONLY ONE PART OF THE INTELLIGENCE CYCLE.
REGARDLESS OF HOW SUCCESSFUL THE "QUESTIONING" MAY BE,
IT IS WORTHLESS UNTIL REDUCED TO WRITING. THE PURPOSE
OF A REPORT IS TO RECORD THE INFORMATION OBTAINED
DURING "QUESTIONING" FOR FUTURE REFERENCE, ANALYSIS
AND DISSEMINATION.

II. RAW NOTES

A.   RAW NOTES INCLUDE:

- WRITTEN NOTES MADE DURING THE "QUESTIONING".
- AUDIO AND VIDEO RECORDINGS OF THE "QUESTIONING".
- ANY DOCUMENTS THE SUBJECT WAS REQUIRED TO FILL
OUT.

B.   THE "QUESTIONER'S" WRITTEN NOTES:

- SHOULD BE BRIEF.
  SHOULD BE MADE AS SURREPTITIOUSLY AS POSSIBLE.
- SHOULD BE LABELED WITH DATE/TIME INFORMATION.
- SHOULD NOT DIVULGE AREAS OF INTEREST BY ONLY
TAKING NOTES ON CERTAIN TOPICS.

III. USE OF RECORDING DEVICES

THE FOLLOWING SUGGESTIONS APPLY EQUALLY TO BOTH AUDIO
AND VIDEO RECORDING DEVICES.

A.   THE SUBJECT SHOULD NOT BE AWARE THAT HE IS BEING
RECORDED.

B.   DO NOT ATTEMPT TO RECORD THE ENTIRE "QUESTIONING"
UNLESS THERE IS A SPECIAL PURPOSE FOR DOING SO. SUCH
AS LATER EDITING THE TAPE FOR SPECIAL EFFECTS.

C.   A/C CURRENT IS PREFERABLE TO BATTERIES BUT
BATTERIES SHOULD BE AVAILABLE AS BACKUP.

D.   IF YOU MUST USE BATTERIES, THEN ALWAYS START EACH
SESSION WITH FRESH BATTERIES.

E.   YOU SHOULD HAVE A BACKUP RECORDER IN CASE THE
FIRST MALFUNCTIONS.

F.   PLAN FOR TAPE REPLACEMENT BEFORE STARTING THE
SESSION.

G.   LABEL TAPES ON THE OUTSIDE AND ALSO RECORD AN
IDENTIFYING HEADER ON THE TAPE ITSELF.

IV. PRINCIPLES OF REPORT WRITING

A. ACCURACY - INFORMATION SHOULD BE REPORTED EXACTLY

AS OBTAINED FROM THE SUBJECT. HEARSAY OR "QUESTIONER"

COMMENTS SHOULD BE IDENTIFIED AS SUCH.

B. BREVITY - THE REPORT SHOULD BE BRIEF AND TO THE

, POINT. NOONE WANTS TO READ A TEN PAGE REPORT THAT

COULD HAVE BEEN SUMMED UP IN ONE OR TWO.

C. CLARITY - TAKES PRECEDENCE OVER BREVITY. DON'T

MAKE THE REPORT SO BRIEF THAT IT LACKS PERTINENT

DETAILS.

1. USE SIMPLE SENTENCES AND UNDERSTANDABLE

LANGUAGE.

BE SPECIFIC - DON'T GENERALIZE.

.. AVOID ABBREVIATIONS WHICH ARE NOT COMMONLY

KNOWN. IT O.K. TO ABBREVIATE NAMES OF

ORGANIZATIONS BUT SPELL OUT THE FULL NAME THE

FIRST TIME IT APPEARS IN THE REPORT FOLLOWED BY

THE ABBREVIATION IN PARENTHESES. THEN USE THE

ABBREVIATION THROUGHOUT THE REMAINDER OF THE

REPORT.

D. COHERENCE - REPORT ITEMS IN A LOGICAL, ORDERLY SEQUENCE.

E. COMPLETENESS - ANSWER ALL QUESTIONS WHICH MAY BE ASKED BY THE READER OF THE REPORT. REPORT NEGATIVE ANSWERS TO PREVENT MISUNDERSTANDINGS AND DUPLICATIONS DURING SESSIONS.

F. TIMELINESS - TAKES PRECEDENCE OVER ALL OTHER PRINCIPLES. YOU MUST WEIGH PERISHABILITY OF THE INFORMATION AGAINST COMPLETENESS. IF IT REACHES THE USER TOO LATE, IT IS OF NO VALUE.

V. FORMATS

THERE IS NO SET FORMAT BUT AT A MINIMUM EVERY REPORT SHOULD ANSWER WHO, WHAT, WHEN, WHERE, WHY, AND HOW. THE FOLLOWING ARE GUIDELINES FOR THE FINAL REPORT:

A. ONE TOPIC - ONE REPORT. THIS IS A TREMENDOUS AID IN LATER ANALYSIS, ESPECIALLY WHEN USING COMPUTERIZED CROSS-REFERENCES OR INDEXING.

B. THE REPORT SHOULD RELATE TO SPECIFIC REQUIREMENTS. REMEMBER THAT THE OBJECTIVE OF THE "QUESTIONING" WAS TO MEET THOSE SPECIFIC REQUIREMENTS.

C. THE REPORT SHOULD INCLUDE AN ASSESSMENT OF THE SUBJECT, HIS INTELLIGENCE, EXPERIENCE, COOPERATIVENESS, AND RELIABILITY.

D.   THE REPORT SHOULD INCLUDE A DISCUSSION OF THE

TECHNIQUES USED.   INCLUDE ALL APPROACHES USED, HOW YOU

USED THEM, AND WHICH TECHNIQUE BROKE THE SUBJECT.

E.   THE REPORT SHOULD INCLUDE A RECOMMENDATION

(POSITIVE OR NEGATIVE) FOR ADDITIONAL "QUESTIONING",

BASED UPON THE SUBJECT'S SPECIALIZED AREAS OF

KNOWLEDGE.

K-13   L.   NONSENSE QUESTIONING

TWO OR MORE "QUESTIONERS" ASK THE SUBJECT
QUESTIONS WHICH SEEM STRAIGHTFORWARD BUT WHICH
ARE ILLOGICAL AND HAVE NO PATTERN. ANY ATTEMPTED
RESPONSE BY THE SUBJECT IS INTERRUPTED BY
ADDITIONAL UNRELATED QUESTIONING. IN THIS
STRANGE ATMOSPHERE THE SUBJECT FINDS THAT THE
PATTERN OF THOUGHT WHICH HE HAS LEARNED TO
CONSIDER NORMAL IS REPLACED BY AN EERIE
MEANINGLESSNESS.

AT FIRST HE MAY REFUSE TO TAKE THE QUESTIONING
SERIOUSLY, BUT AS THE PROCESS CONTINUES DAY AFTER
DAY, IT BECOMES MENTALLY INTOLERABLE AND HE
BEGINS TO TRY TO MAKE SENSE OUT OF THE SITUATION.
CERTAIN TYPES OF VERY ORDERLY AND LOGICAL
SUBJECTS BEGIN TO DOUBT THEIR SANITY AND IN THEIR
ATTEMPTS TO CLARIFY THE CONFUSION MAKE
SIGNIFICANT ADMISSIONS AND BETRAY VALUABLE
INFORMATION.

M.   RAPID FIRE QUESTIONING

THE SUBJECT IS ASKED A SERIES OF QUESTIONS IN
SUCH A MANNER THAT HE DOES NOT HAVE TIME TO
ANSWER COMPLETELY BEFORE THE NEXT QUESTION IS
ASKED. BY LIMITING THE TIME HE HAS TO FORMULATE
HIS ANSWERS, HE MAY BECOME CONFUSED AND
CONTRADICT HIMSELF. THE "QUESTIONER" THEN
CONFRONTS HIM WITH THESE INCONSISTENCIES AND IN
MANY INSTANCES, HE WILL BEGIN TO TALK FREELY IN
AN ATTEMPT TO EXPLAIN HIMSELF AND NEGATE THE
"QUESTIONER'S" CLAIM OF INCONSISTENCIES. IN
ATTEMPTING TO EXPLAIN HIS ANSWERS, HE IS LIKELY
TO REVEAL MORE THAN HE INTENDED.

III. CONCLUSION

IT MAY BE NECESSARY FOR THE "QUESTIONER" TO USE SEVERAL
TECHNIQUES TOGETHER OR IN SUCCESSION. HE SHOULD DECIDE
DURING THE PLANNING STAGE WHICH TECHNIQUES MATCH THE
PERSONALITY OF THE SUBJECT AND OF THESE, WHICH WILL WORK
WELL TOGETHER. HE MUST BE PREPARED TO MAKE A SMOOTH
TRANSITION FROM ONE TECHNIQUE TO ANOTHER AS THE SUBJECT'S
WEAKNESSES BECOME APPARENT DURING THE "QUESTIONING". .

COERCIVE TECHNIQUES

I. THE THEORY OF COERCION

A. THE PURPOSE OF ALL COERCIVE TECHNIQUES IS TO
INDUCE PSYCHOLOGICAL REGRESSION IN THE SUBJECT BY
BRINGING A SUPERIOR OUTSIDE FORCE TO BEAR ON HIS WILL

L-2   TO RESIST. REGRESSION IS BASICALLY A LOSS OF
AUTONOMY, A REVERSION TO AN EARLIER BEHAVIORAL LEVEL.
AS THE SUBJECT REGRESSES, HIS LEARNED PERSONALITY
TRAITS FALL AWAY IN REVERSE CHRONOLOGICAL ORDER. HE
BEGINS TO LOSE THE CAPACITY TO CARRY OUT THE HIGHEST
CREATIVE ACTIVITIES, TO DEAL WITH COMPLEX SITUATIONS,
TO COPE WITH STRESSFUL INTERPERSONAL RELATIONSHIPS, OR
TO COPE WITH REPEATED FRUSTRATIONS. *THE USE OF MOST
COERCIVE TECHNIQUES IS IMPROPER AND VIOLATES* ...

L-3   B. THERE ARE THREE MAJOR PRINCIPLES INVOLVED IN THE
SUCCESSFUL APPLICATION OF COERCIVE TECHNIQUES:

L-3   DEBILITY (PHYSICAL WEAKNESS)
FOR CENTURIES "QUESTIONERS" HAVE EMPLOYED VARIOUS
METHODS OF INDUCING PHYSICAL WEAKNESSES:
PROLONGED CONSTRAINT; PROLONGED EXERTION;
EXTREMES OF HEAT. COLD. OR MOISTURE; AND *... THESE TECHNIQUES SHOULD NOT BE*
DEPRIVATION OF FOOD OR SLEEP. ʌ THE ASSUMPTION *... OF THESE TECHNIQUES THAT IS*
THAT LOWERING THE SUBJECT'S PHYSIOLOGICAL
RESISTANCE WILL LOWER HIS PSYCHOLOGICAL CAPACITY
FOR RESISTANCE: HOWEVER. THERE HAS BEEN NO
SCIENTIFIC INVESTIGATION OF THIS ASSUMPTION.

MANY PSYCHOLOGISTS CONSIDER THE THREAT OF

INDUCING DEBILITY TO BE MORE EFFECTIVE THAN

DEBILITY ITSELF. PROLONGED CONSTRAINT OR

EXERTION, SUSTAINED DEPRIVATION OF FOOD OR

SLEEP, ETC. OFTEN BECOME PATTERNS TO WHICH A

SUBJECT ADJUSTS BY BECOMING APATHETIC AND

WITHDRAWING

INTO HIMSELF. IN SEARCH OF ESCAPE FROM THE

DISCOMFORT AND TENSION. IN THIS CASE DEBILITY

WOULD BE COUNTER.PRODUCTIVE.

ANOTHER COERCIVE TECHNIQUE IS

~~THE "QUESTIONER" SHOULD BE CAREFUL~~ TO MANIPULATE

SUCH AS ARRA

~~NOT TO CREATE THEM~~ ~~AMEALS AND SLEEP PATTERNS.~~

SO ~~THEY CCC"~~ IRREGULARLY, IN MORE THAN ABUNDANCE OR
R

LESS THAN ADEQUACY, ON NO DISCERNIBLE TIME

IS DONE

PATTERN. THIS ~~CAN~~ DISORIENT THE SUBJECT AND

~~IT~~ DESTROY ING HIS CAPACITY

TO
RESIST. HOWEVER IF SUCCESSFUL IT CA
SERIOUS PSYCHOLOGICAL DAMAGE USED THERE
IS A SE   TCR NC
DEPENDENCY   C   E
Y

L-4

HE IS HELPLESSLY DEPENDENT UPON THE "QUESTIONER"

FOR THE SATISFACTION OF ALL BASIC NEEDS.

L-5   ~~DREAD (INTENSE FEAR & ANXIETY)~~

SUSTAINED LONG ENOUGH, A STRONG FEAR OF ANYTHING

VAGUE OR UNKNOWN INDUCES REGRESSION. ON THE

OTHER HAND. MATERIALIZATION OF THE FEAR IS

LIKELY TO COME AS A RELIEF. THE SUBJECT FINDS

THAT HE CAN HOLD OUT AND HIS RESISTANCE IS

STRENGTHENED.

~~A WORD ~~ ~~II~~ ~~CAUTION~~: IF THE DEBILITY-DEPENDENCY-

DREAD STATE IS UNDULY PROLONGED, THE SUBJECT MAY

SINK INTO A DEFENSIVE APATHY FROM WHICH IT IS

HARD TO AROUSE HIM. ∧ *THIS ILLUSTRATES WHY THIS*

~~PSYCHOLOGIST AVAILABLE WHENEVER COERCION IS~~ *COERCIVE TECHNIQUE MAY PRODUCE TORTURE*

~~INVOLVED~~. *IT IS ADVISABLE TO HAVE A*

L-6

II. OBJECTIONS TO COERCION

A. THERE IS A PROFOUND MORAL OBJECTION TO APPLYING

DURESS BEYOND THE POINT OF IRREVERSIBLE PSYCHOLOGICAL

DAMAGE SUCH AS OCCURS DURING BRAINWASHING.

BRAINWASHING INVOLVES THE CONDITIONING OF A SUBJECT'S

"STIMULUS-RESPONSE BOND" THROUGH THE USE OF THESE SAME

TECHNIQUES, BUT THE OBJECTIVE OF BRAINWASHING IS

DIRECTED PRIMARILY TOWARDS THE SUBJECT'S ACCEPTANCE

AND ADOPTION OF BELIEFS, BEHAVIOR, OR DOCTRINE ALIEN

TO HIS NATIVE CULTURAL ENVIRONMENT FOR PROPAGANDA

RATHER THAN INTELLIGENCE COLLECTION PURPOSES. *THIS TECHNIQUE* ~~ASIDE~~

~~FROM THIS EXTREME, WE WILL NOT JUDGE THE VALIDITY OF~~

~~OTHER ETHICAL ARGUMENTS.~~ *IS ILLEGAL AND MAY NOT BE USED.*

Moreover

B. ∧ SOME PSYCHOLOGISTS FEEL THAT THE SUBJCT'S ABILITY

L-7   TO RECALL AND COMMUNICATE INFORMATION ACCURATELY IS AS

IMPAIRED AS HIS WILL TO RESIST. ~~THIS OBJECTION HAS~~

~~SOME VALIDITY BUT THE USE OF COERCIVE TECHNIQUES WILL~~

~~RARELY CONFUSE A RESISTANT SUBJECT SO COMPLETELY THAT~~

~~HE DOES NOT KNOW WHETHER HIS OWN CONFESSION IS TRUE OR~~

~~FALSE. HE DOES NEED MASTERY OF ALL HIS MENTAL AND~~

~~PHYSICAL POWERS TO KNOW WHETHER HE IS A SPY OR NOT.~~

ON A CONFESSION IS OBTAINED. THE CLAS SIC CAUTI ONS

APPLY HE PRESSURES ARE LIFTED ENOUGH SO THAT THE

SUBJECT CA ROVIDE INFORMATION AS ACCURATELY AS

POSSIBLE N P

. THE RELIEF GRANTED THE SUBJECT AT

THIS POINT FITS NE LY INTO THE "QUESTIOING" PLAN. HE

IS TOLD THAT THE CHANGED TREATMENT IS A REWARD FOR

TRUTHFU NESS AND EVIDENC THAT FRIENDLY HANDLING WILL

C Dn NUE AS LONG AS HE COOPERATES.

III. JUSTIFICATION FOR USING COERCIVE TECHNIQUES

THESE TECHNIQUES SHOULD BE RESERVED FOR THOSE SUBJECTS
WHO HAVE BEEN TRAINED OR WHO HAVE DEVELOPED
THE ABILITY TO RESIST NON-COERCIVE TECHNIQUES.

L-8 IV. COERCIVE TECHNIQUES

A. ARREST

L-8

THE MANNER AND TIMING OF ARREST SHOULD BE PLANNED TO

ACHIEVE SURPRISE AND THE MAXIMUM AMOUNT OF MENTAL

DISCOMFORT. HE SHOULD THEREFORE BE ARRESTED AT A

MOMENT WHEN HE LEAST EXPECTS IT AND WHEN HIS MENTAL

AND PHYSICAL RESISTANCE IS AT ITS LOWEST. IDEALLY IN THE

EARLY HOURS OF THE MORNING. WHEN ARRESTED AT THIS TIME,

MOST SUBJECTS EXPERIENCE INTENSE FEELINGS OF

SHOCK, INSECURITY, AND PSYCHOLOGICAL STRESS AND FOR

THE MOST PART HAVE GREAT DIFFICULTY ADJUSTING TO THE

SITUATION. IT IS ALSO IMPORTANT THAT THE ARRESTING

PARTY BEHAVE IN SUCH A MANNER AS TO IMPRESS THE

SUBJECT WITH THEIR EFFICIENCY.

L-9   B. ' DETENTION

- cut hair   A PERSON'S SENSE OF IDENTITY DEPENDS UPON A CONTINUITY
- issue
  baggy   IN HIS SURROUNDINGS, HABITS, APPEARANCE; ACTIONS,
  clothing
        ·   RELATIONS WITH OTHERS, ETC. DETENTION PERMITS THE

             "QUESTIONER" TO CUT THROUGH THESE LINKS AND THROW THE

             SUBJECT BACK UPON HIS OWN UNAIDED INTERNAL RESOURCES.

             DETENTION SHOULD BE PLANNED TO ENHANCE THE SUBJECT'S

             FEELINGS OF BEING CUT OFF FROM ANYTHING KNOWN AND.

             REASSURING.

             LITTLE IS GAINED IF CONFINEMENT MERELY REPLACES ONE

             ROUTINE WITH ANOTHER. THE SUBJECT SHOULD NOT BE

             PROVIDED WITH ANY ROUTINE TO WHICH HE CAN ADAPT.

             NEITHER SHOULD DETENTION BECOME MONOTONOUS TO THE

             POINT WHERE THE SUBJECT BECOMES APATHETIC. APATHY IS

             A VERY EFFECTIVE DEFENSE AGAINST "QUESTIONING".

             CONSTANTLY DISRUPTING PATTERNS WILL CAUSE HIM TO

             BECOME DISORIENTED AND TO EXPERIENCE FEELINGS OF FEAR

             AND HELPLESSNESS.

             IT IS IMPORTANT TO DETERMINE IF THE SUBJECT HAS BEEN

             DETAINED PREVIOUSLY, HOW OFTEN, HOW LONG, UNDER WHAT

             CIRCUMSTANCES, AND WHETHER HE WAS SUBJECTED TO

             "QUESTIONING". FAMILIARITY WITH DETENTION OR EVEN

             WITH ISOLATION REDUCES THE EFFECT.

L-10   C.   DEPRIVATION OF SENSORY
              STIMULI

SOLITARY CONFINEMENT ACTS ON MOST PERSONS AS A

POWERFUL STRESS.   A PERSON CUT OFF FROM EXTERNAL

STIMULI TURNS HIS AWARENESS INWARD AND PROJECTS

HIS UNCONSIOUS OUTWARD.   THE SYMPTOMS MOST

COMMONLY

PRODUCED BY SOLITARY CONFINEMENT ARE SUPERSTITION,

INTENSE LOVE OF ANY OTHER LIVING THING, PERCEIVING

INANIMATE OBJECTS AS ALIVE, HALLUCINATIONS AND

DELUSIONS.   ~~SYMTONS OF A SERIOUS IMPROPRIETY AND
DELIBERATELY CAUSING STRESS~~

~~ALTHOUGH~~ CONDITIONS   IDENTICAL TO THOSE OF SOLITARY

CON INEMENT FO
                R THE PURPOSE OF "QUESTIONING" HAVE NOT

BEEN DUPLICATED FOR SCIENTIFIC EXPERIMENTATION, A

NUMBER OF EXPERIMENTS HAVE BEEN CONDUCTED WITH

SUBJECTS WHO VOLUNTEERED TO BE PLACED IN "SENSORY

DEPRIVATION TANKS".   THEY WERE SUSPENDED IN WATER AND

WORE BLACK-OUT MASKS, WHICH ENCLOSED THE ENTIRE HEAD

AND ONLY ALLOWED BREATHING.   THEY HEARD ONLY THEIR OWN

BREATHING AND SOME FAINT SOUNDS OF WATER FROM THE

PIPING.

TO use PROLONGED SOLITARY CONFINEMENT
    FOR THE PURPOSE of EXTRACTING
    INFORMATION in QUESTIONING   VIOLATE POLIC
                                        S   Y.

~~TO SUMMARIZE THE RESULTS OF THESE EXPERIMENTS:~~

EXTREME

1) A DEPRIVATION OF SENSORY STIMULI INDUCES STRESS AND
ANXIETY. ~~THE MORE COMPLETE THE DEPRIVATION, THE MORE~~ _AND IS A FORM OF TORTURE. I TS UNCONSTITUES_ _UNBEARB(L)_ _A SER IOUS_ _MPROPRIETY AND_
~~RAPIDLY AND DEEPLY THE SUBJECT IS AFFECTED.~~ _VIOLATES POLICY._

THE STRESS AND ANXIETY BECOME UNBEARABLE FOR MOST

2) SUBJECTS. THEY HAVE A GROWING NEED FOR PHYSICAL _A_ ND

SOCIAL STIMULI. HOW MUCH THEY ARE ABLE TO STAND

DEPENDS UPON THE PSYCHOLOGICAL CHARACTERISTICS OF THE

INDIVIDUAL. NOW LET ME RELATE THIS TO THE

"QUESTIONING" SITUATION. AS THE "QUESTIONER" BECOMES

LINKED IN THE SUBJECT'S MIND WITH HUMAN CONTACT AND

MEANINGFUL ACTIVITY, THE ANXIETY LESSENS. THE

"QUESTIONER" CAN TAKE ADVANTAGE OF THIS RELATIONSHIP

BY ASSUMING A BENEVOLENT ROLE.

3) SOME SUBJECTS PROGRESSIVELY LOSE TOUCH WITH

REALITY, FOCUS INWARDLY, AND PRODUCE DELUSIONS,

HALLUCINATIONS AND OTHER PATHOLOGICAL EFFECTS. IN

GENERAL, THE MORE WELL-ADJUSTED A SUBJECT IS, THE MORE

HE I S AFFECTED BY DEPRIVATION. NEUROTIC AND PSYCHOTIC

SUB JECTS ARE COMPARATIVELY UNAFFECTED OR SHOW

DECREASES IN ANXIETY.

D.   THREATS AND FEAR

THE THREAT OF COERCION USUALLY WEAKENS OR DESTROYS
RESISTANCE MORE EFFECTIVELY THAN COERCION ITSELF. FOR
EXAMPLE, THE THREAT TO INFLICT PAIN CAN TRIGGER FEARS
MORE DAMAGING THAN THE IMMEDIATE SENSATION OF PAIN.
IN FACT, MOST PEOPLE UNDERESTIMATE THEIR CAPACITY TO
WITHSTAND PAIN. IN GENERAL, DIRECT PHYSICAL BRUTALITY
CREATES ONLY RESENTMENT, HOSTILITY, AND FURTHER
DEFIANCE.

THE EFFECTIVENESS OF A THREAT DEPENDS ON THE
PERSONALITY OF THE SUBJECT, WHETHER HE BELIEVES THE
"QUESTIONER" CAN AND WILL CARRY OUT THE THREAT, AND ON
WHAT HE BELIEVES TO BE THE REASON FOR THE THREAT. A
THREAT SHOULD BE DELIVERED COLDLY, NOT SHOUTED IN
ANGER, OR MADE IN RESPONSE TO THE SUBJECT'S OWN
EXPRESSIONS OF HOSTILITY. EXPRESSIONS OF ANGER BY THE
"QUESTIONER" ARE OFTEN INTERPRETED BY THE SUBJECT AS A
FEAR OF FAILURE, WHICH STRENGTHENS HIS RESOLVE TO
RESIST.

A THREAT SHOULD GRANT THE SUBJECT TIME FOR COMPLIANCE
AND IS MOST EFFECTIVE WHEN JOINED WITH A SUGGESTED
RATIONALIZATION FOR COMPLIANCE. IT IS NOT ENOUGH THAT
A SUBJECT BE PLACED UNDER THE TENSION OF FEAR; HE MUST
ALSO DISCERN AN ACCEPTABLE ESCAPE ROUTE.

THE THREAT OF DEATH HAS BEEN FOUND TO BE WORSE THAN

USELESS. THE PRINCIPAL REASON IS THAT IT OFTEN

INDUCES SHEER HOPELESSNESS; THE SUBJECT FEELS THAT HE

IS AS LIKELY TO BE CONDEMNED AFTER COMPLIANCE AS

BEFORE. SOME SUBJECTS RECOGNIZE THAT THE THREAT IS A

BLUFF. AND THAT SILENCING THEM FOREVER WOULD DEFEAT THE

"QUESTIONER'S" PURPOSE.

THE PRINCIPAL DRAWBACK TO USING THREATS
~~IF A SUBJECT REFUSES TO COMPLY ONCE A THREAT HAS BEEN~~
PHYSICAL COERCION OR TORTURE IS THAT
~~MADE, IT MUST BE CARRIED OUT. IF IT IS NOT CARRIED~~
THE SUBJECT MAY CALL THE BLUFF. IF H ✓
~~OUT, THEN SUBSEQUENT THREATS WILL ALSO PROVE~~
DOES, AND SINCE SUCH THREATS CANNOT BE
~~INEFFECTIVE~~
CARRIED OUT, THE USE OF EMPTY THREATS
COULD RESULT IN SUBJETE GAINING RATHER

L-12   E. PAIN THAN LOSING SELF-CONFIDENCE,

EVERYONE IS AWARE THAT PEOPLE REACT VERY DIFFERENTLY

TO PAIN BUT THE REASON IS NOT BECAUSE OF A DIFFERENCE

IN THE INTENSITY OF THE SENSATION ITSELF. ALL PEOPLE

HAVE APPROXIMATELY THE SAME THRESHOLD AT WHICH THEY

BEGIN TO FEEL PAIN AND THEIR ESTIMATES OF SEVERITY ARE

ROUGHLY THE SAME. THE WIDE RANGE OF INDIVIDUAL

REACTIONS IS BASED PRIMARILY ON EARLY CONDITIONING TO

PAIN.

THE TORTURE SITUATION IS AN EXTERNAL CONFLICT, A

CONTEST BETWEEN THE SUBJECT AND HIS TORMENTOR. THE

PAIN WHICH IS BEING INFLICTED UPON HIM FROM OUTSIDE

HIMSELF MAY ACTUALLY INTENSIFY HIS WILL TO RESIST. ON

THE OTHER HAND, PAIN WHICH HE FEELS HE IS INFLICTING

UPON HIMSELF IS MORE LIKELY TO SAP HIS RESISTANCE.

FOR EXAMPLE, IF HE IS REQUIRED TO MAINTAIN RIGID

POSITIONS SUCH AS STANDING AT ATTENTION OR SITTING ON

A STOOL FOR LONG PERIODS OF TIME. THE IMMEDIATE SOURCE

OF ~~PAIN~~ *DISCOMFORT* IS NOT THE "QUESTIONER" BUT THE SUBJECT

HIMSELF. HIS CONFLICT IS THEN AN INTERNAL STRUGGLE.

AS LONG AS HE MAINTAINS THIS POSITION. HE IS

ATTRIBUTING TO THE "QUESTIONER" THE ABILITY TO DO

SOMETHING WORSE. BUT THERE IS NEVER A SHOWDOWN WHERE

THE "QUESTIONER" DEMONSTRATES THIS ABILITY. AFTER A

PERIOD OF TIME. THE SUBJECT ~~IS LIKELY TO~~ *MAY* EXHAUST HIS

INTERNAL MOTIVATIONAL STRENGTH. *THIS TECHNIQUE MAY ONLY BE USED FOR PERIODS OF TIME THAT ARE NOT LONG ENOUGH TO INDUCE PAIN OR PHYSICAL DAMAGE* INTENSE PAIN IS QUITE LIKELY TO PRODUCE FALSE

CONFESSIONS, FABRICATED TO AVOID ADDITIONAL

PUNISHMENT. THIS RESULTS IN A TIME CONSUMING DELAY

WHILE INVESTIGATION IS CONDUCTED AND THE ADMISSIONS

ARE PROVEN UNTRUE. DURING THIS RESPITE. THE SUBJECT

CAN PULL HIMSELF TOGETHER AND MAY EVEN USE THE TIME TO

DEVISE A MORE COMPLEX CONFESSION THAT TAKES STILL

LONGER TO DISPROVE.

SOME SUBJECTS ACTUALLY ENJOY PAIN AND WITHHOLD

INFORMATION THEY MIGHT OTHERWISE HAVE DIVULGED IN

ORDER TO BE PUNISHED.

IF PAIN IS NOT USED UNTIL LATE IN THE "QUESTIONING"
PROCESS AND AFTER OTHER TACTICS HAVE FAILED. THE
SUBJECT IS LIKELY TO CONCLUDE THAT THE "QUESTIONER" IS
BECOMING DESPARATE. HE WILL FEEL THAT IF HE CAN HOLD
OUT JUST A LITTLE LONGER. HE WILL WIN THE STRUGGLE AND
HIS FREEDOM. ONCE A SUBJECT HAS SUCCESSFULLY
WITHSTOOD PAIN. HE IS EXTREMELY DIFFICULT TO
"QUESTION" USING MORE SUBDUED METHODS.

L-13   F.   HYPNOSIS AND HEIGHTENED SUGGESTIBILITY

THE RELIABILITY OF ANSWERS OBTAINED FROM A SUBJECT
ACTUALLY UNDER THE INFLUENCE OF HYPNOTISM IS HIGHLY
DOUBTFUL. HIS ANSWERS ARE OFTEN BASED UPON THE
SUGGESTIONS OF THE "QUESTIONER" AND ARE DISTORTED OR
FABRICATED.

HOWEVER. THE SUBJECT'S STRONG DESIRE TO ESCAPE THE
STRESS OF THE SITUATION CAN CREATE A STATE OF MIND
WHICH IS CALLED HEIGHTENED SUGGESTIBILITY. THE
"QUESTIONER" CAN TAKE ADVANTAGE OF THIS STATE OF MIND
BY CREATING A "HYPNOTIC SITUATION", AS DISTINGUISHED
FROM HYPNOSIS ITSELF. THIS HYPNOTIC SITUATION CAN BE
L-14   CREATED BY THE "MAGIC ROOM" TECHNIQUE.

FOR EXAMPLE. THE SUBJECT IS GIVEN AN HYPNOTIC
SUGGESTION THAT HIS HAND IS GROWING WARM. HOWEVER,
HIS HAND ACTUALLY DOES BECOME WARM WITH THE AID OF A
CONCEALED DIATHERMY MACHINE. HE MAY BE GIVEN A
SUGGESTION THAT A CIGARETTE WILL TASTE BITTER AND HE
COULD BE GIVEN A CIGARETTE PREPARED TO HAVE A SLIGHT
BUT NOTICEABLY BITTER TASTE.

A PSYCHOLOGICALLY IMMATURE SUBJECT, OR ONE WHO HAS
BEEN REGRESSED, COULD ADOPT A SUGGESTION THAT HE HAS
BEEN HYPNOTIZED, WHICH HAS RENDERED HIM INCAPABLE OF
RESISTANCE. THIS RELIEVES HIM OF THE FEELING OF
RESPONSIBILITY FOR HIS ACTIONS AND ALLOWS HIM TO
REVEAL INFORMATION.

L-15   H.   NARCOSIS

THERE IS NO DRUG WHICH CAN FORCE EVERY SUBJECT TO
DIVULGE ALL THE INFORMATION HE HAS, BUT JUST AS IT IS
POSSIBLE TO CREATE A MISTAKEN BELIEF THAT A SUBJECT
HAS BEEN HYPNOTIZED BY USING THE "MAGIC ROOM"
TECHNIQUE. IT IS POSSIBLE TO CREATE A MISTAKEN BELIEF
THAT A SUBJECT HAS BEEN DRUGGED BY USING THE "PLACEBO"
L-16   TECHNIQUE.

STUDIES INDICATE THAT AS HIGH AS 30 TO 50 PERCENT OF
INDIVIDUALS ARE PLACEBO REACTORS. IN THIS TECHNIQUE
THE SUBJECT IS GIVEN A PLACEBO (A HARMLESS SUGAR PILL)
AND LATER IS TOLD HE WAS GIVEN A TRUTH SERUM, WHICH
WILL MAKE HIM WANT TO TALK AND WHICH WILL ALSO PREVENT
HIS LYING. HIS DESIRE TO FIND AN EXCUSE FOR
COMPLIANCE, WHICH IS HIS ONLY AVENUE OF ESCAPE FROM
HIS DEPRESSING SITUATION, MAY MAKE HIM WANT TO BELIEVE
THAT HE HAS BEEN DRUGGED AND THAT NO ONE COULD BLAME
HIM FOR TELLING HIS STORY NOW. THIS PROVIDES HIM WITH
A RATIONALIZATION THAT HE NEEDS FOR COOPERATING.

THE FUNCTION OF BOTH THE "PLACEBO" TECHNIQUE AND THE
"MAGIC ROOM" TECHNIQUE IS TO CAUSE CAPITULATION BY THE
SUBJECT, TO CAUSE HIM TO SHIFT FROM RESISTANCE TO
COOPERATION. ONCE THIS SHIFT HAS BEEN ACCOMPLISHED,
THESE TECHNIQUES ARE NO LONGER NECESSARY AND SHOULD
NOT BE USED PERSISTENTLY TO FACILITATE THE
"QUESTIONING" THAT FOLLOWS CAPITULATION.

IV.

REGRESSION

AS I SAID AT THE BEGINNING OF OUR DISCUSSION OF

COERCIVE TECHNIQUES, THE PURPOSE OF ALL COERCIVE

TECHNIQUES IS TO INDUCE REGRESSION. HOW

SUCCESSFUL THESE TECHNIQUES ARE IN INDUCING

REGRESSION DEPENDS UPON AN ACCURATE PSYCHOLOGICAL

ASSESSMENT OF THE

L-17   ~~THERE ARE A FEW PROPER MATCHING TECHNIQUES TO SOURCE~~ ALSO

~~WHICH~~ ~~USED~~ TO INDUCE REGRESSION, BUT ~~TO A LESSER DEGREE THAN~~ IT IS ILLEGAL AND

AGAINST POLICY TO USE THEM TO PRODUCE

~~CAN BE OBTAINED WITH COERCIVE TECHNIQUES. THE~~

~~EFFECTIVENESS OF THESE TECHNIQUES DEPENDS UPON THE~~

~~REGRESSION~~ ~~FOLLOWING~~ IS HARD IS REAL

~~"QUESTIONER'S" CONTROL OF THE ENVIRONMENT. FOR~~ AS I SUSCEPTIBILITY

~~EXAMPLE:~~ ~~THESE~~ ~~CARE~~ BE ~~TO ABUS~~ O F THEIR

E : CAUSE

A. PERSISTENT MANIPULATION OF
    TIME
B. RETARDING AND ADVANCING CLOCKS SERVING

C. MEALS AT ODD TIMES

D. DISRUPTING SLEEP SCHEDULES

E. DISORIENTATION REGARDING DAY AND

F. ~~UNPAT~~ UNPATTERNED "QUESTIONING" SESSIONS

G. NONSENSICAL QUESTIONING

H. IGNORING HALF-HEARTED ATTEMPTS TO
    COOPERATE

I. REWARDING NON-COOPERATION

IN GENERAL, THWARTING ANY ATTEMPT BY THE SUBJECT TO

RELATE TO HIS NEW ENVIRONMENT WILL REINFORCE THE

EFFECTS OF REGRESSION AND DRIVE HIM DEEPER AND

DEEPER INTO HIMSELF, UNTIL HE NO LONGER IS ABLE TO

CONTROL HIS RESPONSES IN AN ADULT FASHION.

WHETHER REGRESSION OCCURS SPONTANEOUSLY UNDER

INADVERTENTLY)

DETENTION OR IS ~~INDUCED~~ BY THE "QUESTIONER". IT ~~SHOULD~~ *CALLS*

FOR REMEDIAL TREATMENT AS SOON AS IT IS NOTICED.

~~NOT BE ALLOWED TO CONTINUE BEYOND THE POINT NECESSARY~~

IN A CS

~~TO OBTAIN COMPETENCE.~~ A ~~PSYCHIATRIST~~ SHOULD BE *CALLED.*

ESENT IF SEVER TECHNIQUES   O

PR   E   ARE TO BE EMPLOYED, T

INSURE FU LL REVERSA L LATER. AS SOON AS POSSIBLE, THE

QUESTIO NER" SHOULD PROVIDE THE SUBJECT WITH THE

RATIONALIZATION THAT HE NEEDS FOR GIVING IN AND

COOPERATING. THIS RATIONALIZATION IS LIKELY TO BE

ELEMENTARY, AN ADULT VERSION OF A CHILDHOOD EXCUSE

SUCH AS:

1. "THEY MADE YOU DO IT."

2. "ALL HE OTHER BOYS ARE DOING IT."

3. "YOU'RE REALLY A GOOD BOY AT HEART. '

Made in the USA
Las Vegas, NV
26 September 2024

95816514R00070